WITHDRAWN

HOOKED ON
HANDWORK

Design a Rug Inspired by Fibers, Textiles, and Handcrafts

KATHLEEN ECKHAUS

Ampry Publishing, Northbrook, Illinois

Copyright © 2022 by Ampry Publishing LLC
Published by
AMPRY PUBLISHING LLC
3400 Dundee Road, Suite 220
Northbrook, IL 60062
www.amprycp.com

www.rughookingmagazine.com
Graphic design by Matt Paulson

All rights reserved, including the right to reproduce the book or portions thereof in any form or by any means, electronic or mechanical, including photocopying, recording, or by any information storage and retrieval system, without permission in writing from the publisher. All inquiries should be addressed to Rug Hooking Magazine, 3400 Dundee Road, Suite 220, Northbrook, IL 60062.

Printed in the United States of America
10 9 8 7 6 5 4 3 2 1

Rug photos and photos of handwork by the artists, unless otherwise noted
Cover photographs by the author
All other photography by the author
Cataloging-in-Publication Data

Library of Congress Control Number: 2022935504

ISBN 978-1-945550-60-7

Dedication

Mel Eckhaus, photography assistant

I started writing this book in 2020, the year that my 50th wedding anniversary had to be postponed, the year that my husband and I spent more time together than we had in our 50 years of marriage, and the year that significantly reinforced my understanding that I am married to a good man. We met in college and married after graduation. Together we spent three years teaching in Malaysia for the Peace Corps and raised four children who are now raising families of their own. Together we now visit grandchildren and delight in watching them grow. Together we are planning to travel more, hike more, dance more, and enjoy our home and our hobbies more. Here's to you, Mel Eckhaus. I couldn't have found a better partner!

Acknowledgments

From the bottom of my heart, I want to thank all the talented rug hookers who shared their work in this book. Some of them already had a design that was based on a quilt or a piece of needlework and in these pages tell the story of its creation. Others found something to use as inspiration, got out their markers, and came up with a brand-new design. The artists in this book range from beginners to masters in the field of rug hooking. Some have published articles in *Rug Hooking* magazine; others have been recognized in exhibits with their prize-winning creations. Several contributors were my students who were willing to jump in and create an original piece as their second project. They borrowed cutters and dug through donated bags of wool strips to help demonstrate to readers that each of us can design a rug, no matter what level of experience.

Special shoutouts to: Karen Larsen and Tracy Granger for donating materials; Karen for steaming and binding rugs for some of us who don't like to finish projects; Karen, Peg McPherson, and Jennika Borger for reviewing these pages to make certain that all was in order; Brigitte Webb and others who pointed me in the direction of talented rug hookers that I had never met; Laura Baumgardner for providing inspiration pieces; Ellen Banker for alerting me to the Open Access and Creative Commons resources; Larry Hinton, master woodworker, for the fabulous frame that now surrounds the cat rug; and lastly, thank you to my favorite editor and cheerleader, Debra Smith. Deb and I met when our children were little; we discovered early-on that we both delighted in all things textile. We have traveled together to Scotland, Peru, and England, and we have plans to travel some more so that we can ooh and aah at local artwork and handcrafts in far-off places. It's been a friendship of sharing our love of reading, music, and fibers, and we still share those interests. Thank you, Deb, for giving me this opportunity.

Table of Contents

Acknowledgments .... *iii*

Introduction *1*

Chapter 1: Knit and Crochet 5

Chapter 2: Pieced Quilts 18

Chapter 3: Appliqué 26

Chapter 4: Weaving 42

Chapter 5: Needlework 66

Chapter 6: Other Rugs 90

Chapter 7: Fabric Prints 98

Chapter 8: Other Handcrafts.. 108

Chapter 9: Inspiration from The Gambia... 122

Conclusion..*124*

Resources and References *125*

List of Contributing Artists *126*

Introduction

Don't think about making art, just get it done. Let everyone else decide if it's good or bad, whether they love it or hate it. While they are deciding, make even more art. — *Andy Warhol*

I grew up in the countryside of Western Pennsylvania where my family raised pansies to sell, vegetables to can, and rabbits to eat. My mother made most of my clothing, had a candy-making business, and decorated cakes professionally. My dad plowed the fields for planting and taught me how to weed and hoe.

My grandparents on both sides did all that, too, so it makes sense that I became one of those people who likes to make everything from scratch. Back in our homesteading days, raising our family in the country, we grew our own vegetables, and I canned and preserved our food. We raised goats for milk and chickens for eggs. I made garments for all of us.

Sometime in the 1970s, I took a rug-hooking class. As a beginner, not quite understanding rug hooking yet, I just couldn't leave empty holes in the foundation cloth, so I packed my loops too tightly; my mat was stiff as a board. I learned. Then I started over and learned to make softer pieces, creating small wall hangings for my friends. It wasn't long until I was teaching wall hanging classes and warning students not to pack those loops. I didn't make my first actual rug until I joined the Magdalena Rug Hookers of Perry County, Pennsylvania, in 2011. Now I have a wool stash that has taken over several closets and a couple of large wooden chests.

When I started rug hooking, it never occurred to me to buy a design on linen. My first rugs and mats were simple hearts and scallops. Later I added sleeping chipmunks and menopausal mermaids, all designed on my own.

From two of the author's rugs: Above, a sleeping chipmunk snoozes beneath a mushroom. Below, her menopausal mermaid rug.

I do not call myself an artist, but I can copy a photo or an object fairly well. I often draw something on paper and then cut it out and trace around it on the linen. There are usually multiple versions of every motif until I get it the way I want it. Even my less-than-marvelous drawings turn into lovable hooked rugs. I've given some away, and I have places in my home where I cycle through my collection, changing the rugs throughout the year. Even if I don't love everything about a rug, it is still usable.

Many fiber artists are like me and find the faults in their own work and this is often why they don't have the courage to design. As a rug-hooking teacher, one of my frustrations at the end of a beginner class is that lack of confidence in designing. Most students leave with total self-assurance in the rug-hooking process, but do not think they have the artistic ability to come up with their own patterns. I tell them that I am not an artist either, and suggest things like using coloring books or children's drawings for ideas. But for most of them, their next project is probably going to be one that is already drawn on the linen.

My beginning hooking class always includes information about Magdalena Briner Eby, who lived in the county where I now live. (More about her later.) Magdalena's rugs are simple designs, and she didn't try to make them perfect. If she ran out of a certain color of wool, she finished the motif with something else. She hooked birds without feet and horses with red eyes right up by their ears. Was she an artist? Her work today is revered in the rug-hooking world as some of the finest primitive art of her time. And if she can make a sweet rug, I think my new students can, too.

During class introductions, it is evident that most of my students already pursue other fiber and textile arts, and now they want to try something new. They are passionate and self-assured about the things they already do but have trepidation about rug-hooking design. What would help them realize that they are as capable of designing a rug as they are of planning their other projects?

At our local rug-hooking group, I noticed that several quilters were hooking rugs that looked like patchwork, and I wondered if I could engage and excite other quilters, weavers, and knitters in the same way. What if they could create a hooked piece that is complementary to another textile art that they already enjoy?

I started to pay attention to the rugs that popped up on social media and found many examples of designs based on other textiles and fiber arts. Now if I could just convince new rug hookers to give that a try.

This book is not a "how-to" volume—it is simply filled with examples of hooked pieces that are inspired by other art forms. Most of these inspirations are based on textile and fiber arts, but I could not stop there. Some of my students have been potters or jewelry makers, so I added a miscellaneous design chapter based on non-textile creations.

If you are a new rug hooker, use these examples to motivate you to create your own designs based on the arts you already love. If you are an experienced designer, I hope these examples will get your creative juices flowing. If rug hooking is the only fiber art you pursue, I suspect you enjoy the designs of weavers, knitters, quilters, and other artists. Pay attention to what pleases you and see if you can incorporate the same elements in your rugs.

Inspiration is not copying. Look at the way your favorite artist uses colors. Look at how the motifs are placed. Did someone make a rug to match a tablecloth in their kitchen? You could do that! Did another rug hooker design a rug to match living room couch pillows? You could do that! A hooked rug that is designed by another is not for us to copy, but getting ideas, walking away, and then designing something of our own is how we grow and become better artists.

The world of textile art is vast, and I have only scratched the surface. In writing this book, I contacted rug hookers from around the globe to see what inspires their rug designs. I learned many things by reading about their experiences, and I hope you do, too. These are their stories.

TRACY GRANGER

Lollipop Bouquet, *mixed fibers on burlap on linen. Designed and hooked by Magdalena Briner Eby, Perry County, Pennsylvania, ca. 1881. Courtesy of Traditions by Wright & Co., Oxford, Ohio.*

Vertical Crow, Horse, and Duck, *28" x 44", mixed fibers on burlap or linen. Designed and hooked by Magdalena Briner Eby, Perry County, Pennsylvania, ca. 1880. Photo courtesy of Traditions by Wright & Co., Oxford, Ohio.*

Author's Note

Most of the rugs in this book were designed by the artists. There are, however, some that were made from purchased designs. I added these to the book as examples so readers can see other arts that adapt readily to a hooked rug. I am not opposed to purchased patterns and I have used some myself; I just want everyone to know that they can design a personal rug if they so desire.

1 Knit and Crochet

Properly practiced, knitting* soothes the troubled spirit, and it doesn't hurt the untroubled spirit either.
— Elizabeth Zimmermann

* and crocheting (revision to Elizabeth's quote by the author)

Knitting and crocheting fascinate me. If you gave me two needles or a hook and a ball of yarn, I would never have come up with either. But someone did, and that happened a long time ago. Since knitted and crocheted items are fragile; it is impossible to determine when the techniques were developed. We will never know the complete history of either, but both ancient arts are still popular today.

Knitting and crochet differ from an ancient textile art, weaving, in that they are a single length of yarn that is looped in rows upon itself. Weaving requires fibers going over and under each other in opposing directions. To get the intricate designs found in knitted and crocheted items, the artist must employ several different stitches that cause the yarn to twist upon itself in particular ways that form designs and patterns.

Inspiration: Argyle Knitting

Not all diamonds are created equal. Some have more flaws than others, but don't we love them all? Never a fan of argyle sweaters or socks, I took this on as a challenge. I enjoy hooking a geometric pattern on rug warp, and argyle is simply diamonds—wonderful diamonds! What started as a monochromatic mat from my stash of creams, grays, and blacks soon evolved into a color palette of amber and garnet. My wool dyed with men's silk ties introduced the garnet, giving me added value. Drawing the pattern was easy. I just counted threads to keep everything straight and perfectly aligned.

This was my first attempt at hooking with wool yarn. I chose a hand-dyed nubby style that added to the challenge to hook straight lines. Since every rug takes on a personality of its own, I surrendered to that and allowed the yarn to guide my journey. Accepting the unique personality of this mat let me enjoy the process much more. I finished it by whipping the edge to a wool fabric backing, creating a pillow.

— Tracy Granger

Author's Note

The argyle design comes from the tartan of the Campbell Clan from the county of Argyll in western Scotland. Authentic Campbell tartan is woven of green, blue, and black fabric in a distinct pattern that is also referred to as Black Watch tartan. In the sixteenth century, woven tartan fabric was cut on the bias to add stretch before it was fashioned into socks.

Argyle sweater inspiration

Auditioning the Stash III, Argyle Study: Diamonds Are a Girl's Best Friend, *17½" x 29", off-the-bolt wool, silk-tie-dyed wool, hand-dyed Downeast Woolly yarn by Heidi Wulfraat, Nova Scotia. Designed and hooked by Tracy Granger, East Stroudsburg, Pennsylvania, 2020.*

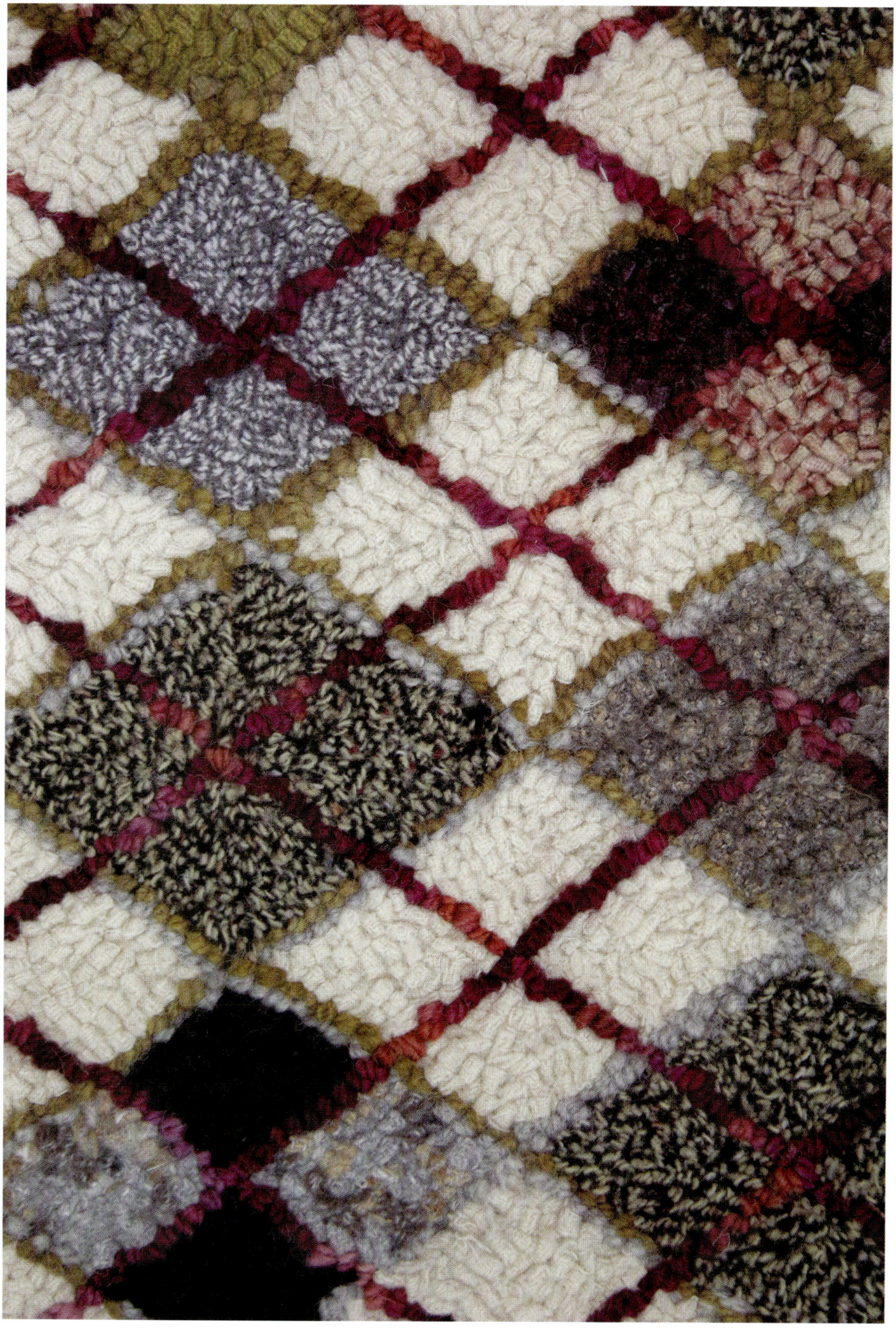

KATHLEEN ECKHAUS

Detail, **Diamonds are a Girl's Best Friend**

Inspiration: Fragments of a Knitted Sweater

My first exposure to rug hooking was when I was in Decorah, Iowa. I had been invited to the Norwegian-American Museum in 1998 to teach weaving and felting. In one room, there were two ladies demonstrating rug hooking. I asked them to show me how this rug hooking was done. They were happy to show me something that they said I would be able to learn to do in fifteen minutes. That was right, because that was all the teaching I ever received related to rug hooking.

Since then, I have designed and hooked rugs as a way to express myself. I like to think I can tell stories that people find interesting. Rug hooking is not known in Norway, so there is only a little group around me who have learned the craft.

I learned knitting from my grandmother when I was a child. She had hoped to teach the craft to a sweet granddaughter, but she had only grandchildren who were boys. She tried to teach all of us, but I was the only one who took to it and continued to knit.

Many years ago, I found in a book a photo of an old sweater that was in a museum in Norway. It was probably made in 1846. I got a couple of photographs from the museum so I could reconstruct the sweater. I knit one for myself and wore it for many years. When it became too small for me, my daughter wore it, and now it is lying in the bottom of a wooden chest waiting for somebody new to use it.

Recently, I decided to make a rug inspired by that sweater. I took a section of the pattern from the front of the sweater and used it for the design of the rug. I took a picture of that section, then used a light table to copy the lines on to transparency film. I used an overhead projector to project it on the backing and then drew the pattern with a marker.

I intended to use black and white wool to look like the original sweater, but as I began to work on the rug, I could not resist adding colors. I have chosen to lighten the pattern toward the edge to give the illusion that the rug is old and in the process of fading.

My advice to others who want to use knitting patterns in rug design is don't count squares to try to make an exact copy. It will be stiff and dull and there will be no life in the rug. Use the knitting as an inspiration and let the pattern be more alive, with some variations and bulky lines.

—Håkon Grøn Hensvold

Inspiration sweater knit by Håkon Grøn Hensvold, Skreia, Norway

Fragments, *26" x 19", wool yarn on rug warp. Designed and hooked by Håkon Grøn Hensvold, Skreia, Norway, 2020.*

Inspiration: Crocheted Afghan

I wish I could say that I have an intriguing background, like searching for yarn in Morocco by hot-air balloon, but my professional life as an auditor was devoid of excitement and individuality. That made it even more important for me to find pursuits to satisfy my need for creativity and color.

My grandma taught me to crochet when I was about five years old, and though I've learned so many other fiber arts over the years, only crocheting takes me back to the treasured moments spent at my grandparents' farm. I am happy when I have a crochet project to work on in my basket. For Christmas one year, my husband gave me a kit to crochet Jane Crowfoot's *Persian Tiles* afghan in the Eastern Jewels colorway designed by Lucia Dunn. I was immediately drawn in by the gorgeous, cheerful colors and the intricate details of the pattern. Despite decades of experience, I had never made anything like this and admit to being intimidated, but it was so pretty that I had to try—and now it's one of my all-time favorites!

I thought the octagonal motif of this afghan would make a beautiful hooked table mat but was concerned by the challenge of changing the complex crochet pattern into something I could hook. First, I enlarged a copy of the crochet chart to the size I wanted my rug to be. Then I used a permanent marker to outline the most important elements, simplifying without losing the overall design effect. To transfer the pattern, I traced these lines on tulle with permanent marker, then laid the tulle pattern on top of monk's cloth and traced again. This was my first experience using tulle in this way, and I was pleasantly surprised by how well it worked and how inexpensive it was. After some color planning, hooking was the easiest part, and the small rug worked up quickly. To finish, I bound the edges with a bulky black wool yarn.

Still considering myself a beginner rug hooker, I learn something from every project. This project taught me the value of using the right wool for the design. My choices were based on color—I purchased wool that was beautifully dyed by a local fiber store. What I didn't consider was that the wool, with its loose, plaid structure, wasn't well suited to the smaller #4 and #6 cuts I used in the rug. The edges frayed, some strips broke while hooking, and it didn't hold its shape well next to the stiffer black wool. While it's not perfect, I'm pleased that the final rug does resemble the stunning crochet pattern that inspired it.

—Julia Majury

Jane Crowfoot's **Persian Tiles** *afghan in the Eastern Jewels colorway designed by Lucia Dunn. Crocheted by Julia Majury, Elliottsburg, Pennsylvania.*

Eastern Jewels Rug, *12" octagon, #4- and 6-cut wool on monk's cloth. Inspired by Jane Crowfoot's* Persian Tiles *afghan in the Eastern Jewels colorway designed by Lucia Dunn. Hooked by Julia Majury, Elliottsburg, Pennsylvania, 2021.*

Inspiration: Grandma's Traditional Granny Squares

I've always admired hooked rugs, especially the primitive folk-art types with animals and/or geometric designs. When my fiber arts guild had Kathy Eckhaus come to teach a workshop, I thought I had died and gone to heaven! In the class, I worked on a kit with the drawing on linen and all the wool strips provided. As soon as it was finished, I was ready to start my own. Kathy suggested I base my design on some other fiber art that was pleasing to me.

I chose a Granny Square afghan because my grandmother made them all the time. Her vision was failing, but she could crochet the blocks by feel and was always taking everyone's scrap yarns to use up. (The only yarn we bought for her was the black for edges and highlights.) I loved that they were scrappy and resembled stained glass.

I designed my rug to have the blocks on the diagonal, which made the hooking a real challenge for a newbie. It was difficult to make a straight line and to keep the blocks the same size. I tried hard to reproduce the actual rings of segmented color but failed miserably, so I went with random patterns of color and tried to keep all the blocks different. For the borders, I used some of all the colors and then added messages to inspire myself to behave well.

I used a variety of sizes of wool strips, since I was using up scraps from the workshop (#8 cut) and from a friend who gave me her stash (smaller than #8). I bought a used cutter but couldn't seem to get it to cut through the wool fabric, so I cut strips with a ruler and rotary cutter. I bought a couple of pieces of dyed wool from a fabric store that carries wool for rug hookers, I stripped a pair of trousers from the local thrift shop, and my aunt gave me an old coat to use when she found out I was into rug making. (I'm beginning to sound a bit like my grandmother!)

I know my rug is not perfect, but I am in love with the whole process, and I can't wait to do more! I have lots of inspiration from all the other things that I or family members have made. Maybe my next hooking will look like a table runner I wove. Time will tell.

—Francie Appleman

Granny Square afghan crocheted by Elizabeth Nolf Bell, Shippenville, Pennsylvania, 1972

Grandma's Tradition, 23½" x 31½", #6- and 8-cut wool on linen.
Designed and hooked by Francie Appleman, Turbotville, Pennsylvania, 2020.

Inspiration: Filet Crochet

The name of the crochet pattern is *Hearts-in-the-Round Runner*. I especially liked that it was narrow and worked up quickly. Someone suggested that it would make a pretty rug design, so I enlarged the design, then traced it on linen using my light box. I didn't want the rug to be too long, so I omitted some of the hearts.

I must say I did not like hooking all the small areas that were only a couple of loops long—too much starting and stopping! But I do think this is a pretty rug and I am happy to have it displayed near my crocheted runner.

—Peg McPherson

Author's Note

Filet crochet designs are usually made using two types of stitches that form either filled or empty blocks. The filled sections make up the motif and the empty areas become the background. For a translation into a hooked piece, consider enlarging the motifs so that there will be less stopping and starting if you want to avoid Peg's challenge.

Filet crochet hearts

Hearts in the Round, *10½" x 30½", #10 crochet thread. Designed by Donna Piglowski and crocheted by Peg McPherson, New Bloomfield, Pennsylvania, 2019.*

Filet Crochet, *12" x 31½", #8-cut wool on linen. Designed and hooked by Peg McPherson, New Bloomfield, Pennsylvania, 2021.*

Inspiration: Lace (and Ruth Bader Ginsburg)

It was her lace jabot that captured me. That and the feisty strength of the woman. Wouldn't it be fun to do a rug to honor her? But I do not hook portraits, so I didn't think too much more about it. Not long after I had those thoughts, I saw that The Old Tattered Flag had a pattern called *Grandmother's Lace*. I was drawn to it because I love all kinds of needlework. But I hesitated, not wanting to buy the pattern because I really didn't need another project.

When a few friends and I decided to work on a joint challenge inspired by the "notorious" Ruth Bader Ginsburg, I had the perfect reason to buy the pattern I had been lusting over. I had The Old Tattered Flag make the pattern slightly larger so that I could adapt it into my own RBG design, and I hooked away at that lace jabot.

Notorious RBG died about the time we finished our challenge; I like to think she would have approved.

—Debra Smith

Creative Tip

The basis for the RBG rug on the facing page is a purchased pattern featuring a lace doily. But any lace pattern could be enlarged, adapted, drawn on linen, and incorporated into a rug design.

Closeup of handmade lace from Spain. Any type of lace can inspire a hooked rug. Make it simpler than the actual lace but keep a lacy effect.

RBG, *50" x 60", #4- to 8-cut wool on linen. Adapted from a design by The Old Tattered Flag and hooked by Debra Smith, Landisburg, Pennsylvania, 2019.*

2 Pieced Quilts

You can't use up creativity. The more you use, the more you have. — *Maya Angelou*

I suspect a lot of us grew up with patchwork quilts that kept you warm at night or while curled up on the couch reading a book. We often think of quilts as those made by our grandmothers and great-grandmothers from worn-out clothing and scraps of fabric. But there are modern-day quilters piecing together brand-new cloth to make table runners, bed coverings, and wall hangings that range from simple patchwork to extraordinary works of art.

There are multiple categories of quilts, but any of them can be used to inspire hooked rugs. Do you have some family heirlooms, or are you a quilter yourself? Do you love the look of patchwork or log cabin quilts? Let's find out what some artists did using quilts as their inspiration.

LAURA BAUMGARDNER

Inspiration: Pieced Quilt Blocks

I wanted to make a rug that was simple but pretty, so I based my design on two quilt squares. Although I have never made a quilt, my sister is a quilter. I asked her for advice, and she suggested two particular squares from a Better Homes and Gardens publication, *101 Full-Size Quilt Blocks and Borders*. I photocopied the squares, and it was simple to put the design on the linen using my light box. The hooking was straightforward. Once I had the design on the linen, all I had to do was plan the colors. There are 99 more block ideas in the book. I see some future rugs—but I don't intend to do them all!

I have donated this rug to my church's silent auction. I'm sure it will bring in hundreds of dollars! (I wish!) 🙂

— Peg McPherson

Home is Where the Heart Is, *22" x 12", mostly #8-cut wool on linen. Inspired by a design from* 101 Full-Size Quilt Blocks and Borders *(Better Homes and Gardens Books, 1998) and hooked by Peg McPherson, New Bloomfield, Pennsylvania, 2020.*

Inspiration: Log Cabin Quilt

I was inspired to hook this rug by one of my favorite quilt patterns, the Log Cabin. The design is created by placing light and dark fabrics in particular ways to look like stacked logs in a cabin wall. I have a large log-cabin quilt hanging in my living room that I made years ago. I thought a rug with a similar design would complement that quilt.

It took me a very long time to hook *Furrows*, but I love the finished rug. I am a member of the Magdalena Rug Hookers in Perry County, Pennsylvania, and I included this rug in my group's Modern Magdalena exhibit in 2018 at our local arts council. I was delighted by how three-dimensional it looked hanging on the wall.

In the quilting world, the red center of a log cabin block represents the hearth of the home; in this rug, the hearth is hooked with wool yarn instead of fabric strips.

—Lin Keller

Inspiration piece: log cabin quilt created by Lin Keller, Shermans Dale, Pennsylvania

Creative Tip

There are many log cabin quilt designs, and they vary on the way the light and dark pieces are lined up. Look online or in quilting books to see the amazing variety of designs you can achieve with light and dark values.

Furrows, 24" x 36", #8-cut wool on linen using as-is and hand-dyed wool and yarn. Designed and hooked by Lin Keller, Shermans Dale, Pennsylvania, 2017.

Inspiration: Geometric Quilting

This piece was one of my early rug hooking projects and is based on a contemporary quilt design. I attended a class called Quilts to Rugs, taught by Cindy MacIntosh. She provided the class with a variety of books and images to inspire the students to design their own pieces based on quilts. Being a new rug hooker, I chose a design that was not too complicated. The design was hand-drawn by me on the backing. I used mostly recycled wool and some new wool in the borders.

—Tanya McNutt

A Crooked Mile, *pieced by Laurie Baumgardner, 2022*

Geometric Trees Wall Hanging, *20" x 38", #5-cut wool on linen. Designed and hooked by Tanya McNutt, Truro, Nova Scotia, Canada, 2007.*

Pieced Quilts | 23

Inspiration: Geometric Quilt

I enjoy hooking large geometric patterns on rug warp. The quilt pattern, *All Stacked Up*, would allow me to create movement with the choice of light, medium, and dark wools, while still being able to add some eye candy. In my opinion, some of my selections worked better than others.

Unlike many rug hookers, I don't precut a bunch of wool worms before I start hooking. Instead, I cut as I go. If I do have an extra wool strip or two, I have a large piece of rug warp with a geometric design of 3" x 3" blank squares drawn on it, ready for me to use up any leftovers. (More on that later.)

I originally planned (measured and drew) this rug to be 67" x 54" because I had a space on my floor where I wanted it to go—and because I had a lot of wool to audition. But as I was hooking, when I got as far as completing a section 31½" x 54", I started to question my decision. Maybe this rug was big enough. Will it be too busy if I continue? I realized that if I was asking myself those questions, it was time to stop. Luckily, the section I had hooked was a nice rectangle, so trimming the extra rug warp was easy. Now this rug resides at a hallway intersection where it is enjoyed and walked on daily. (The whipped edge was also an audition from my wool yarn stash, but that's another story.)

If you feel your stash is going to outlive you, you may want to try this pattern to help get it back to a manageable size—and there will still be plenty left to touch and admire.

P.S. In 2020, my local art association, the Pocono Arts Council, did a virtual, members-only art exhibit. I hesitated to enter my rug because I had doubts about it and felt it might not be good enough. (Typical thoughts of an artist, right?) Not only was a fiber-art entry recognized, but it also won Best of Show. I was humbled to receive this honor, and yes, I walk on that prize-winning rug every day!

—Tracy Granger

All Stacked Up *quilt pattern. Copyright of the design and layout is owned by Colourwerx. Photo courtesy of Linda & Carl Sullivan, of Colourwerx.*

Best in show!

Auditioning the Stash II, *31½" x 54", #5-cut as-is and overdyed wool on rug warp. Adapted from a design by Free Spirit Quilt Patterns. Hooked by Tracy Granger, East Stroudsburg, Pennsylvania, 2020.*

3 Appliqué

Have nothing in your houses that you do not know to be useful or believe to be beautiful. — William Morris

The term appliqué derives from French and Latin words that mean "to attach." In the world of fiber arts, appliqué had a humble beginning as a way to patch garments and add strength to the worn areas. But humans make beauty wherever they can, and soon patching by adding additional fabric became a way to add decorations to quilts, blankets, and clothing in many cultures around the world.

The Arts and Crafts movement was born in the nineteenth century from the values of people concerned about the effects of industrialization on design and traditional craft. In response, architects, designers, craftsmen, and artists turned to new ways of living and working, pioneering new approaches to create decorative arts.

One of the most influential figures during this time was William Morris, a British designer of more than 600 styles of wallpaper, textiles, tapestries, and carpets, and more than 150 stained-glass windows. He actively promoted the joy of craftsmanship and became recognized across the globe as an artist and craftsman.

Previous examples of appliqué would most likely have been rendered in cotton. But there were also bed, table, and floor rugs made of appliquéd wool. On the bed, this dense fabric would help keep family members warm on cold winter nights. Penny rugs are a distinct style and are so-named because the design consists of wool circles (pennies) layered in decreasing sizes. These were often embellished with embroidery and sometimes had lamb's-tongue, lamb's-ear, or pen-wiper borders. Often these simple appliqué designs were embellished with colorful embroidery.

Inspiration: William Morris

This design was taken from a book titled *Floral Abundance: Appliqué Designs Inspired by William Morris*, by Rosemary Makhan. Rosemary was a Canadian textile artist who specialized in quilting and won many awards for her beautiful creations. She wrote this book using William Morris designs in the public domain and included stencils to make them easily accessible. I copied the motifs that I wanted and transferred the images to red-dot tracing fabric and then to linen backing.

I made my design using the original size of the stencils, but they can be enlarged or reduced in size. This was an easy way to make a beautiful rug that I will enjoy for many years. I added a fabric sleeve to the back and inserted a wooden slat. This rug now hangs from the brickwork of my fireplace and covers the opening. It makes for a pretty fireplace cover.

—Tanya McNutt

William Morris Fireplace Screen, *32" x 32", #3-, 4- and 5-cut mostly-new 100 percent wool on linen. Background wool is spot-dyed by the artist with Majic Carpet Seal Brown. Design inspired by artwork from* Floral Abundance, *by Rosemary Makhan. Hooked by Tanya McNutt, Truro, Nova Scotia, Canada, 2020.*

Inspiration: Sunbonnet Sue with Sam

Sunbonnet-clad little girls have been used in quilts and embroidery since the 1800s but became wildly popular after Bertha Corbett Melcher published a book, *The Sunbonnet Babies*, in 1900. Since their faces are covered by bonnets, they are easy to embroider and appliqué. There were nine more books in the series, written by Eulalie Osgood Grover and illustrated by Bertha Corbett Melcher, and in 1905, Melcher wrote *The Overall Boys*. Many of these books were used as early readers in schools across the country. While I grew up calling Sue's friend just plain Sam, I recently learned he had other names, including Suspender Sam, Sunbonnet Sam, and Overall Bill.

I don't know the history of this doll-bed cover; it was handed down to me and I never thought to ask. Each Sam or Sue is on an individual square, and the squares were pieced together to make the little blanket. Were the squares part of a larger quilt? Was there a plan to make a bigger quilt and no one got around to finishing it? I'll never know.

The doll bed belonged to my mother, and I loved playing with my Tiny Tears doll and covering her with the blanket. Maybe my mom did the same.

A little rug to go beside the bed would be fun for my grandchildren when they come to play. It was easy to transfer the shapes of the figures to my linen with the use of a light box. I traced them as they were, but since it looked like they were walking, I added a road and some flowers and sunshine. I was going for simplicity, like a child's coloring book.

—Kathleen Eckhaus

Sunbonnet Sue

Sam

Appliqué quilt top, unknown maker

Sunbonnet Sue with Sam, *20" x 14", #8-cut wool on linen.
Designed and hooked by Kathleen Eckhaus, Elliottsburg, Pennsylvania, 2020.*

Inspiration: Appliqué Mat

A local friend of mine, Rosalie Furlong, is a well-known quilt designer and maker, artist, and retired art teacher. I chose one of her appliquéd quilt squares and, with her consent, I had her design drawn on linen backing by another superb artist friend of mine, Kevin O'Neil. As rug hookers often do, I wanted to give this design my own interpretation, mostly by using different colors, but also by leaving out some elements and changing others, while still maintaining Rosalie's original design.

It was fun to collaborate with a dear friend. This little hooking reminds me of Rosalie, and that makes me happy.

—Brigitte Webb

Inspiration piece designed and sewn by Rosalie Furlong, Dingwall, Scotland

Garden Bird, *15" x 15", #4- to 7-cut wool on linen.
Adapted from a design by Rosalie Furlong; rug designed and hooked by Brigitte Webb,
Dingwall, Scotland, 2020.*

Inspiration: Kaleidoscope Appliqué

Several years ago, I made a wool appliqué piece from a kit created by WoolyLady. It was an explosion of lovely bright colors, sure to brighten the dark days of winter. When I was finished with the piece, I was not finished with the idea of the kaleidoscope rendered in zappy brights, so I decided to go large. After looking at my stash of wool, I knew that with a bit of judicial dyeing I would have enough wool to hook a similar rug-sized design for my floor. It was a good exercise in color planning, dyeing, values, and hooking points.

—Debra Smith

Appliqué pillow design by WoolyLady

Wool Appliqué, *40" x 40", #6- to 8-cut wool on linen.*
Inspired by a design by WoolyLady and hooked by Debra Smith, Landisburg, Pennsylvania, 2017.

Inspiration: Appliqué Pillow

In the mid-1980s, I was a young mom with two daughters and liked sewing items for my girls and for their dolls. Quilting was popular at the time, and I jumped in with both feet. I bought a precut kit for a Delectable Mountain quilt, and I was smitten! Through the years, being part of Juniata Valley Quilters Guild (Pennsylvania) and attending quilt shows from my home state to Illinois, I took classes on hand-appliqué and wool appliqué and found I totally enjoyed the handwork involved in both.

Paging through wool appliqué books I've collected, I came upon a wool appliqué pillow with geraniums in flowerpots. I pictured this pillow as a hooked rug that would look beautiful in a garden shed or a sun porch.

After starting the rug, I decided the geraniums weren't "popping" the way they did in the picture I had, and I remembered the proddy method of hooking I learned when making an earlier needlework piece, so I applied that technique to this project.

—Christie Yorks

Potted Geranium Pillow. *Design in* **Summer Gatherings** *in by Lisa Bongean and Carol Charles. Wool appliqué by Laura Baumgardner, Mifflintown, Pennsylvania.*

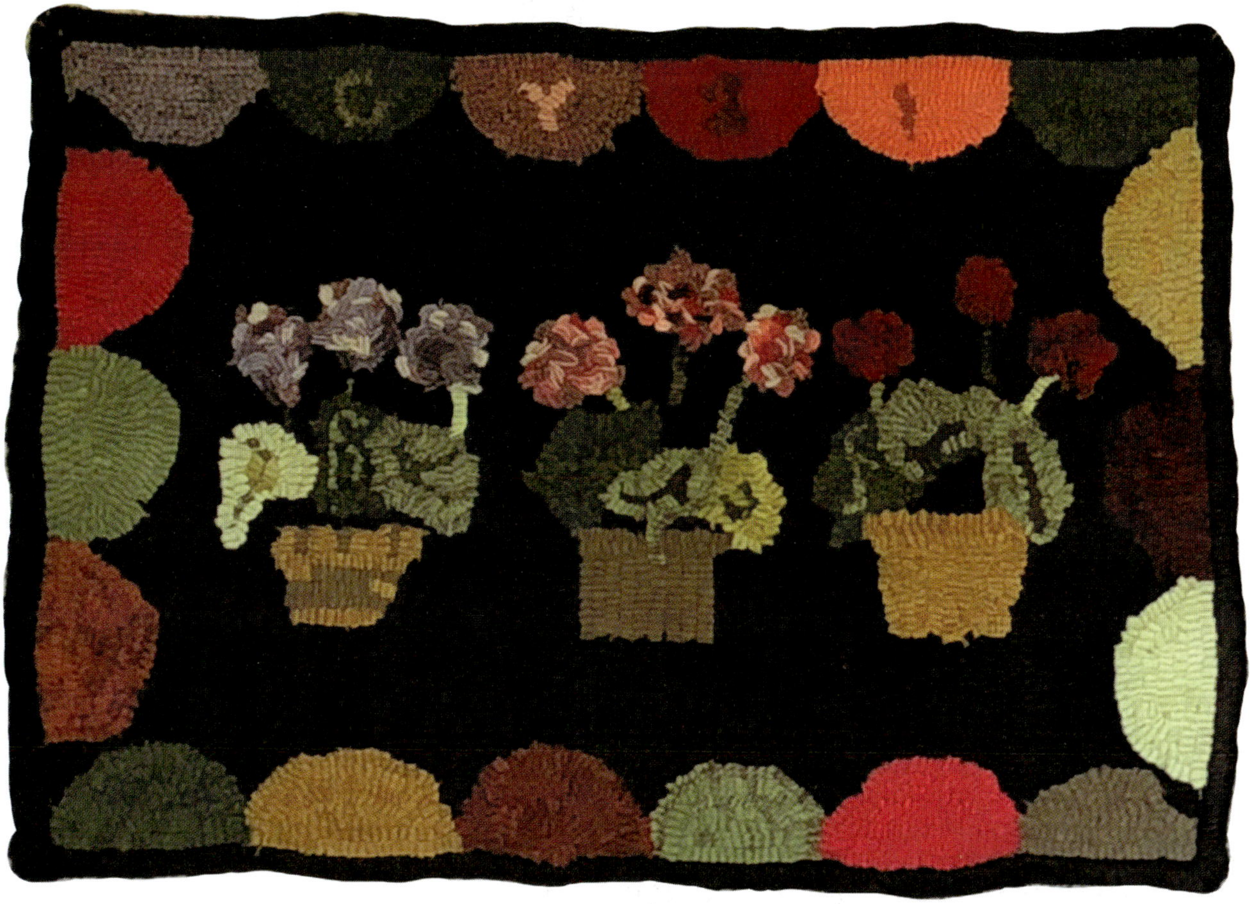

KATHLEEN ECKHAUS

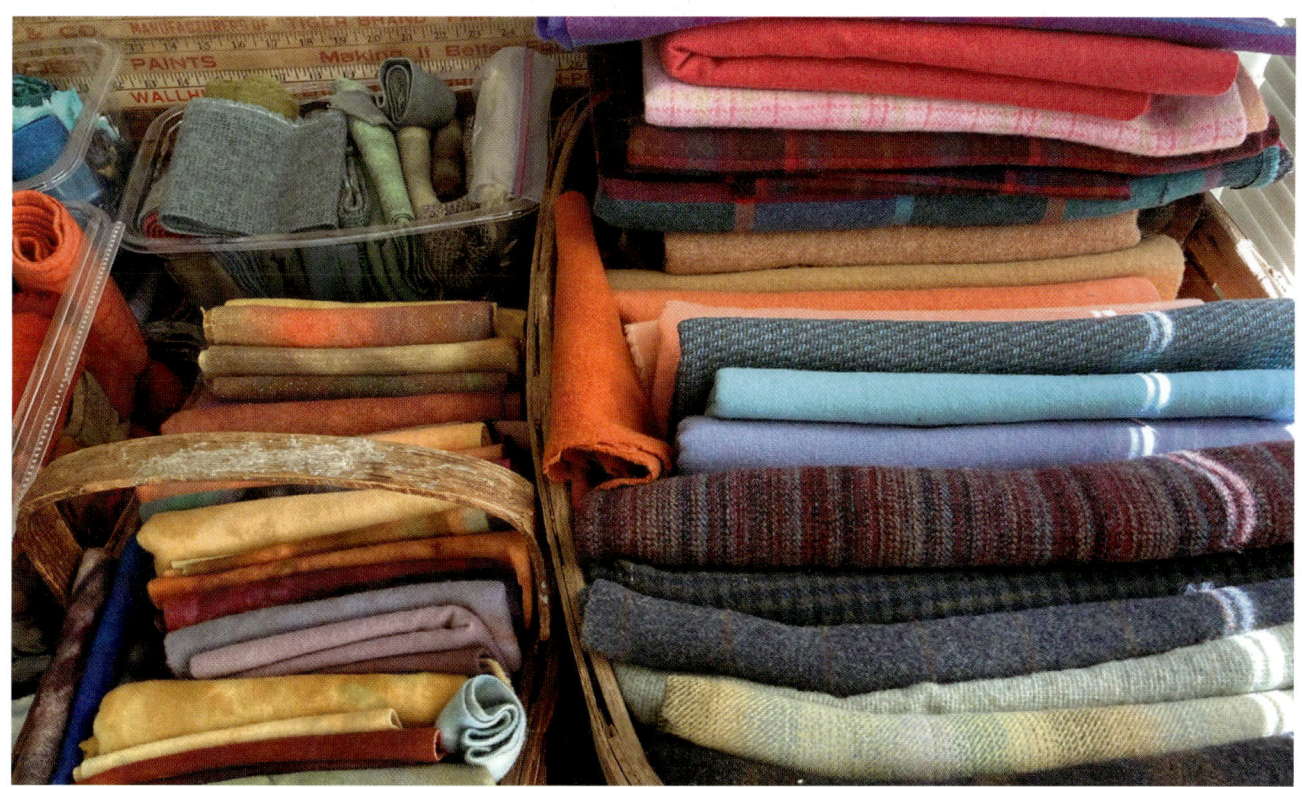

Pretty Posies, *16" x 23", #8-cut wool and proddy flowers on linen. Designed and hooked by Christie Yorks, Mexico, Pennsylvania, 2021.*

TRACY GRANGER

Inspiration: Penny Rug

I have always loved penny rugs, but I never finished one—and I'm not sure that I ever will. That's why I decided to hook one using some of my favorite colors.

Penny rugs are a distinct style and are named because the design consists of wool circles (pennies) layered in decreasing sizes. These were often embellished with embroidery and sometimes had lamb's-tongue, lamb's-ear, or pen-wiper borders.

This is an easy rug to design. Just pick a drinking glass to trace around for the largest penny. Using #8 cut, I hooked one circle around for that penny. The second layer was another row of a single color, and then I finished the middle with a third color for the final penny. You will have to find the middle of your linen and make some decisions about where to place your circles. If you make a mistake, grab another color marker and make the correction. I had to do that a couple of times.

The shapes on my end borders are lambs' ears to me. That name makes me think of something warm and fuzzy. I wouldn't want lambs' tongues or inky pen wipers on my table, so I'll stick with the ears.

A traditional penny rug would have embroidery around the edges of the pennies and often in the middle of the top one. Sometimes the center of the rug would be an appliquéd or embroidered picture. Pansies are my favorite flower, so I added them to the center design. I'm not sure if they represent appliqué or embroidery, but I like the way they look in the middle of this rug.

—Kathleen Eckhaus

COLLEEN MACKINNON

Pennies from Heaven, *20" x 23", #8-cut wool on linen.
Designed and hooked by Kathleen Eckhaus, Elliottsburg, Pennsylvania, 2020.*

Inspiration: Mola

The needlework technique for creating molas is reverse appliqué: the project starts as a stack of different-colored fabrics, and the needleworker very carefully cuts down through the layers to expose each fabric, one at a time, creating lines, designs, borders, and motifs. The color exposed depends on how many layers are cut. The edge of each layer is then carefully stitched under to protect the edges. It is a fascinating, if tedious, process. Typically, molas are bright colors against a dark or bright background.

Hooking a mola is so much easier and faster than the actual process of reverse appliqué. And it is ideal for using odds and ends from a stash—bright bits and bobs against a dark background. The design needs to be well-thought-out to reflect the charm of a real mola; with some forethought and planning, your mola can look authentic. Norma Batastini was the artist who brought mola patterns to rug hookers. Recently deceased, she will be missed.

—Debra Smith

Needlework Inspiration from around the World

There are many examples of hooked rugs based on fiber arts of various cultures from around the world, and it is important that rug hookers respect these traditions. Learn about the origins and meanings of designs and motifs. Do not copy. For example, I think Chinese and Japanese characters are beautiful, flowing shapes that would look lovely in a hooked rug. But they have meaning, and I would not want to hook something just because I thought it looked pretty only to learn that the symbol represents something I didn't mean. Ask permission, learn, and be respectful!

Mola blouse panel from the Kuna Indians, Panama, twentieth century; cotton, plain weave, appliqué and reverse appliqué. Photo courtesy of Honolulu Museum of Art, Creative Commons, public domain. Mola originated in Panama with the women of the Kuna or Guna tribe in the San Blas islands. It is still produced by these indigenous people in both Panama and Colombia. To preserve their cultural heritage, mola cloth can only be sold in those two countries.

Mola, 23" x 20", #6- and 8-cut wool on linen.
Designed by Norma Batastini and hooked by Debra Smith, Landisburg, Pennsylvania, 2013.

Appliqué | 39

Inspiration: Quilted Appliqué Wall Hanging

When Kathleen first mentioned hooking rugs based on designs from other textiles mediums, I was intrigued. As a quilter who also enjoys rug hooking, I wondered about translating an art quilt that I had designed into a hooked mat. Additionally, I had taken a lesson in punch-needle rug hooking and was eager to use that method for a new project. I was guided in my project by Simone Vojvodin's book, *Mastering the Art of Punch Needle Rug Hooking: Techniques and Projects* (2021, RHM). A class with quilt artist Gloria Loughman resulted in the basic design of the landscape for the quilt, which consisted of a few strategically placed lines. I finally settled upon drawing a solitary lupine plant in the foreground to complete the scene. This finished quilt was the basis for my punched mat.

I drew the design on monk's cloth. For punch needle, the design is drawn in reverse because you work from the back of the project. As always, it is important to keep the design on the straight grain of the fabric. Monk's cloth has markings that make this easy. For the lupine, I traced my original design from the quilt, cut it out, and traced around it for the mat. I added massed yellow flowers, with definition supplied by variegated yarn. I used a #10 Regular Oxford Punch Needle, and mostly rug-weight wool yarn. The hills in the distance are double strands of worsted-weight yarn used in the #10 needle. My color choices were governed by the yarn I had available, although I purchased a variegated light purple for the lupine, as well as a variegated light green specifically for this mat. Strategic use of the colors in my available variegated yarns made it possible to give movement and depth to the project. I finished the piece by rolling the first row of punching around the sides and sewing the excess monk's cloth to the back.

This was my first attempt at punching a landscape. I learned to divide multicolored and variegated yarn into its component colors in order to achieve a pleasing result. I also found how easy it is to use double strands of yarn and how interesting the result can be. It was a pleasure to take a design and render it in another way. The quilt and the mat are not identical, which is part of what I find pleasing about this project.

—Gloria McPherson

Photo of scenery that inspired the project

Quilted piece that inspired the punch-needle project

Lupines 2, 15" x 16", *wool yarn punched on monk's cloth using a #10 Regular Oxford Punch Needle. Designed and punched by Gloria McPherson, New Bloomfield, Pennsylvania, 2020.*

4 Weaving

To care about weaving, to make weavings, is to be in touch with a long human tradition. We people have woven, first baskets and then cloth, for at least ten thousand years.
— *Phylis Morrison*

Threads going over and under each other in different ways can make an incredible array of patterns. So many possibilities for hooked rug designs.

Interlacing fibers, or weaving, seems to be instinctual in the animal kingdom: think of spider webs, birds' nests, and beaver dams. Ancient people made woven homes, baskets, and clothing. The simplest weave structure involves vertical (warp) and horizontal (weft) threads that interlace with each other to make a fabric. Look closely at a woven tablecloth and you can see how the weft goes over, under, over, under the warp. Change the pattern so that the weft goes over two or more yarns in various sequences, and you get weave structures such as basket weave, twill, herringbone, and many other variations. But how can we make a hooked rug look like a woven one? Here are some examples to get you going.

KATHLEEN ECKHAUS

Inspiration: Tartan

I decided to hook a pillow for my partner, Seoris McGillivray, based on his family tartan. The McGillivray clan fought with Bonnie Prince Charlie at Culloden—in fact, the clan chief died in that battle. There is so much history in this cloth that I knew Seoris would appreciate a hooked version.

I thought this would be an easy piece to hook, but when I looked at the tartan more closely, I realized how intricate it was. After some thought, I decided to hook a simpler version in an impressionistic way so that it would resemble the woven structure. (I did check to make sure that this tartan is a non-copyright design and in the public domain.)

I chose a section of the tartan to hook and asked Seoris to draw up the design for me. I then transferred it to a piece of rug warp backing with a permanent marker. Next, I looked for suitable colors of wool in my stash—only to discover there were none. Although I had purchased Lucy Richards's fabulous Wooly Mason Jar (WMJ) system a few years back, I had never given it a try. Now I had the motivation I needed, so I grabbed a yard of natural Dorr Mill wool and divided it into strips 3" wide by 18" long. Next, I made up the primary WMJ dyes, getting valuable advice from Lucy, and started dyeing. I hand-dyed all the wool for this piece of hooked tartan in my microwave. And it was easy!

I made it into a small cushion. I searched the internet and found a company that would make a scarf in the McGillivray Dress Tartan big enough for me to use as a backing for the cushion. I found a ball of Briggs & Little wool that worked perfectly as binding, and I finished a meaningful gift for my life partner, Seoris McGillivray.

—Brigitte Webb

Hooked pillow with McGillivray kilt

Author's Note

*Nowhere beats the heart so kindly
as beneath the tartan plaid.*
— William Edmondstoune Aytoun

After the Battle of Culloden in 1746, the English government made wearing tartan and carrying weapons illegal. This was an attempt to quell the rebellious clan system. For some time, tartan became a rare sight. But in 1822, when George IV suggested that the Scots should wear their respective tartans to official functions, the interest in this weave structure was resurrected. By then, many of the weavers who knew the patterns had died and it was necessary to reinvent some of the original tartans. Today, tartans must be officially registered with Lyon Court.

McGillivray Tartan, *10" x 10", #3-, 4-, 6-, and 8-cut wool on rug warp. Designed and hooked by Brigitte Webb, Dingwall, Scotland, 2020.*

Clasped-weft Weaving

The weft is the yarn that is woven horizontally. You can see in the photo of the scarf that in clasped-weft weaving, the weft colors only go partway across. The weaver uses two shuttles, each with a different color. At the point where the colors change, the shuttles have been switched and the yarns looped around each other. Each color goes partway across and then doubles back.

Inspiration piece: Handwoven clasped-weft scarf. Designed and woven by Julia Majury, Elliottsburg, Pennsylvania, 2020.

KATHLEEN ECKHAUS

Inspiration: Clasped-Weft Weaving

Always up for learning new things, I started weaving on a rigid-heddle loom during the pandemic. Plain weave was quick and satisfying, but I soon wanted to explore other styles. Clasped weft, while appearing complicated, is a surprisingly simple technique with a great deal of room for individuality. I wove a scarf for my mom's birthday and we both loved how it turned out.

During a trip to Frederick, Maryland, for our anniversary some years ago, my husband and I purchased a homemade, 1970s-era footstool with the most unappealing greenish-tan, cracked vinyl covering. I planned to re-cover it with a hooked rug. Inspired by my weaving, I decided that the clasped-weft style would work well with the simple character of the stool.

Removing the many layers of previous upholstery and a lot of rusty tacks and staples was an adventure. Hiding under the vinyl was crumbling shelf liner, gauze, paper, feed sacks, and even pieces of trouser legs! After a thorough cleaning and sanding, I turned it upside down and traced the edge on tulle. This was an easy way to account for its uneven sides and oddly-angled corners. After drawing another line outside the first to allow enough area to fold over the edges of the stool), I hooked the two colors of my design in a #8 cut. I enjoyed the structure of hooking all in straight lines, contrasted with the freedom of letting the zigzag effect take shape without a pattern.

Getting my hooked piece onto the stool was another challenge. Next time, I will choose a better-quality square or rectangular footstool with overhanging sides for a tidier result. I loved taking something old and worn and giving it a fresh, new look.

—Julia Majury

Ups and Downs, 13½" x 16½", #8-cut wool on monk's cloth.
Designed and hooked by Julia Majury, Elliottsburg, Pennsylvania, 2020.
Refurbished stool ready for use with its makeover.

Inspiration: Woven Plaid

Ah, math to go with my geometric passion. During TIGHR 2015, Laurie Wiles, from Edmonton, Alberta, Canada, taught a class titled Hooking a Plaid. In her class, we assigned each letter of the alphabet a number, then gave each number a color, and hooked the number of rows accordingly. (It's hard to explain, and it isn't necessary to hook a plaid that way. All you must decide is how many rows of each color and then maintain that sequence throughout the rug, horizontally and vertically. Study some plaids and see how they are designed.)

I wanted to make a runner about 10" wide and 64" long. That's where the math came in, to decide how many repeats I would need.

The runner is hooked in four different color palettes to represent the seasons, starting with winter and ending with fall. If I repeated my sequence twice across, it was about 10". To get the length I needed, I repeated each seasonal section twice, and then added one sequence where I mingled the seasonal colors. If you look closely, you can see these transitions. To make it long enough, I ended with a winter/spring mix section that completed the runner and made it continuous.

I started with what would represent the warp threads of a weaving and hooked the entire piece vertically, leaving spaces for the horizontal rows to fill in where I left spaces. To get the effect that you see, where the loops are in opposing directions, you must count threads in your backing to make sure everything is even.

As I said, I hook all the warp first. I pull my first loop on the first row and follow the straight-of-grain by hooking along one thread of the backing. I then leave three holes or five threads, counting carefully, and pull up my second loop. I carry on until I have the number of loops for my pattern. I finish each of these rows, the whole length of the piece, and then go to the beginning and hook my weft.

The weft rows are easier because you can follow the already-hooked rows. Make sure you still count so that the rows are hooked straight. It's very easy to move over rows, and that will throw the whole pattern off. When you turn the piece over, everything will look straight and flat on the back.

Hooking a plaid is best done on rug warp because it is smooth and even—unlike linen, which has thick and thin threads and can have openings of varying sizes between them. To hook this pattern, you must count threads. I pulled a loop and then counted five threads down to pull a second loop. There is more to it, and if you'd like to give it a try, I suggest you contact Laurie and sign up for a class. Perhaps start with a smaller piece. Hooking a plaid is such fun—and it will help you use up your stash.

—Tracy Granger

Example of one of Laurie Wiles's graphs to hook a plaid. Laurie says, "I think of the over-and-under weave as I hook. I always plot the warp and weft on graph paper before I start."

Seasonal Plaids, *10½" x 64", #5-cut as-is wool, overdyed wool, and textures representing seasonal change. Inspired by TIGHR 2015 class with Laurie Wiles, and designed and hooked by Tracy Granger, East Stroudsburg, Pennsylvania, 2020.*

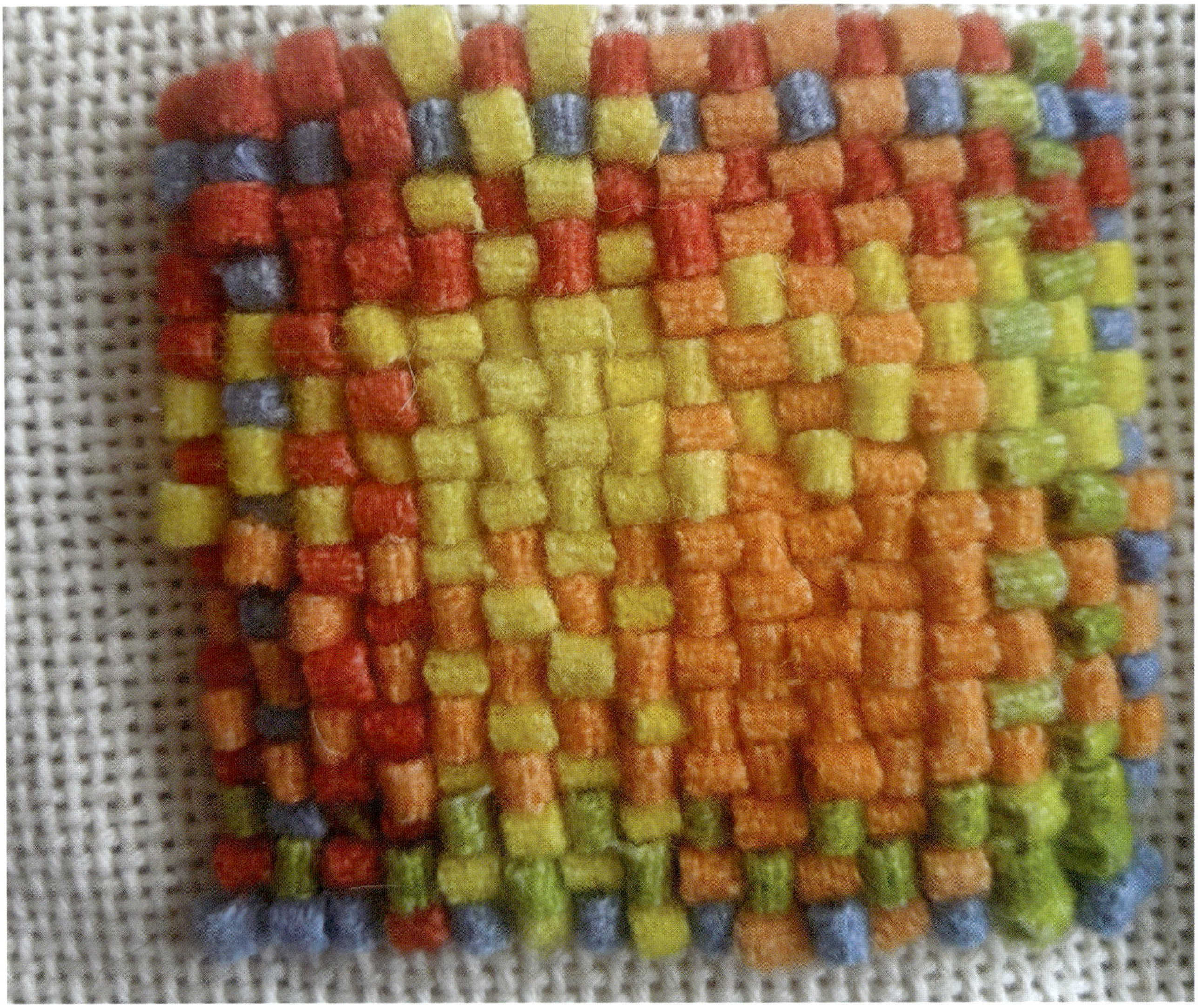

LAURIE WILES

Closeup of hooked plaid showing alternating rows

KATHLEEN ECKHAUS

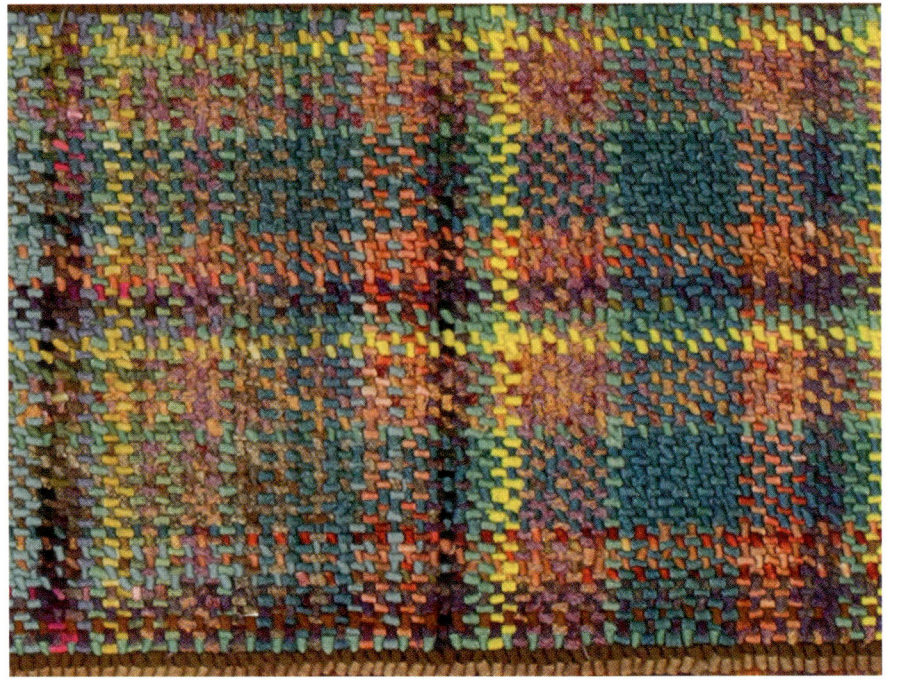

One Way to Manage Your Stash

I have a pretty extensive stash but, unlike my friend Tracy, my stash includes bins and bags of noodles. Unlike Tracy, I cut a bunch before I start a rug and always have a pile of extra. She may have three worms of any one color after she finishes a rug. But what she does next is genius; she takes those leftovers and hooks them into her Worm Catcher Rug. She has a large piece of rug warp that she has divided into squares. When she is done hooking a rug, she takes the handful of worms that she hasn't used and adds them to this rug. It's going to be a big, wonderful rug and, as a result, she doesn't have plastic bags of leftovers like I do. These photos are only a small portion of what each of us really has, but how much tidier my wool collection would be if I didn't have all of those random bags of worms!

KATHLEEN ECKHAUS

KATHLEEN ECKHAUS

TRACY GRANGER

Inspiration: Al-Sadu

Al-Sadu played an important part in Bedouin life in the Middle East. The material was used to provide shelter in the form of Bedouin tents, comfort for saddles when riding camels, carpets and majlis cushions for seating, and to trade. Women would collect fiber from camels, goats, and sheep, then spin yarn that could be dyed using natural pigments and plants, such as henna, turmeric, saffron, cactus, and indigo. Typical colors used in Al-Sadu are black, red, and white. These colors are also found in the UAE flag.

The yarn is woven into fabric, and each has its own unique design. Motifs are often geometric patterns and others that depict common life in the Middle East, such as sand dunes, palm trees, camels, and falcons.

In early Bedouin life, floor looms would have been made of palm or jujube wood: more recently they are available in metal. Floor frames are still in use today, as majlis cushions are still the preferred choice of seating in social settings. In 2011, Al-Sadu was recognized by UNESCO and entered the organization's List of Intangible Cultural Heritage in Need of Urgent Safeguarding.

In this bag, two hooked panels are inspired by Al-Sadu; the leather is from Al Khaznah Tannery in Abu Dhabi and is embroidered to give the impression of Al-Sadu. The zipper tabs feature Telli, traditional embroidery made in Abu Dhabi for the purpose of decorating women's robes. The shoulder strap is fashioned from two agals, a tie-like rope of strings with a tassel on the end (white for regular wear; black and gold for special occasions). Agals are worn by Emirati men on the outside of a traditional headdress, called a gutra. The lining, which is not shown in the photos, is Indian silk with gold and red embroidered motifs; I quilted it to help maintain the bag's internal shape.

I created this bag during an online carpet-bag class with Susan Clarke.

—Ti Seymour

Al-Sadu woven fabric

Front of bag with hooked insert   *Back of bag with hooked piece*   *Zipper tabs featuring traditional embroidery*

Al-Sadu Inspired Bag, *26" x 20", #4- and 5-cut on linen. Designed and hooked by Ti Seymour, Abu Dhabi, UAE, 2021.*

Inspiration: Antique Coverlet

Woven coverlets made of wool, cotton, or linen were popular in the United States in the nineteenth century. Many homes had small looms, and usually women did the weaving. Larger looms and those capable of fancier designs were often owned by professional weavers, usually men, who provided these bed coverings for nearby communities.

Coverlet woven by Leonard Metz, 1842, 8' 9" x 94", Montgomery County, Pennsylvania. Woven of wool and cotton. Photo courtesy of the Metropolitan Museum of Art, New York, New York, Open Access, public domain.

Antique Coverlet, 40" x 45", #8-cut wool on linen.
Designed by The Old Tattered Flag and hooked by Debra Smith, Landisburg, Pennsylvania, 2018.

Several years ago I was a weaver. While I never wove a coverlet, I nevertheless appreciate them and all the work that goes into weaving them. I did not design this rug, though it really is a simple concept—all on a grid, wefts crossing warps. Instead, I purchased the pattern from The Old Tattered Flag, both to support another artist and to allow me to start hooking right away. By the time I was finished pulling loops to create this large rug, I was dying to hook again with colors other than mahogany and cream.

—Debra Smith

Inspiration: Log Cabin Weaving

I am a weaver, and my first hooked rug was from a kit that included all the wool strips. For my second rug, I decided to choose a weaving pattern called Log Cabin and design the rug myself. The log cabin weave structure has been around for a long time. We have seen it used often in quilts.

To put the design on the linen, I just had to decide what size I wanted my blocks to be. I hooked one complete square so that I knew how many loops were used required to fill it. Then I marked off a grid on the rest of the fabric. Once that was done, it was easy to continue hooking the design.

High-contrast colors will make the design pop. They can be different shades of the same color or two totally different colors. You could stay with black as the main color and use multiple colors as the secondary. The size is easily changed since you are working on a grid.

—Susan Kesler-Simpson

Inspiration piece: Handwoven log cabin shawl. Cotton warp and weft, woven on a 4-shaft floor loom. Designed and woven by Susan Kesler-Simpson.

Log Cabin, *16" x 16", #8-cut wool on linen. Designed and hooked by Susan Kesler-Simpson, Danville, Pennsylvania, 2020.*

Inspiration: Ryijy Weaving

In Finland, where I live, there is a style of tapestry weaving called ryijy. Its long tufts create an art form unique to my country. The name ryijy comes from the Scandinavian word rya, which means thick cloth. In the late nineteenth century, ryijy rug weaving developed and became very popular. Some of the most beautiful tapestries were woven then.

Ryijy rugs are similar to tufted, woolen Iranian carpets, but the knots are longer and farther apart. Historically, the Finnish rugs were used as bed coverings and sleigh blankets to keep passengers warm in the winter, and they were made of natural-colored wool. Now they are bright colors with vivid designs—often made to be wall hangings.

I designed this rug to resemble the weaving that surrounded me when I was a child. I added two Alaskan Malamutes (a traditional ryijy weaving might have had wolves) because my family enjoys dog sledding. One of our dogs died recently, and this rug was done before we lost him. Now I'm glad I have this memory of him.

My rug hooking is done using knitted jersey fabric such as old T-shirt material, but for this project, I bought new cloth. My foundation cloth is burlap.

—Sirpa Ojala

Inspiration piece: Traditional Ryijy weaving. Photo courtesy of Suomen Käsityön Ystävät, The Friends of Finnish Handicraft.

Artist Information

Because we live in Finland, where winters are long and cold, we have Alaskan Malamutes. My first Malamute was a big male. He lived almost 14 years and was part of our family. Our other dog is a female and a little smaller. She is a wonderful dog and is now 10 years old. In winter, I go dog sledding around a nearby lake. In summer, our Alaskan Malamute is on holiday, and we row a boat to an island in the lake where the dog can run as much she wants. — Sirpa Ojala

Sirpa Ojala dogsledding

Ryijy Weaving, 23" x 18", *cotton jersey fabric cut into ½" strips, on burlap. Designed and hooked by Sirpa Ojala, Pomarkku, Finland, 2021.*

Inspiration: Saga Nishiki

I wove this mat to resemble the traditional form of Japanese weaving called Saga Nishiki. I am not a weaver, but I admire the beauty of this cloth that is used to make kimono, obi-sash, purses, and other items. It originates in the Saga Prefecture and is a time-consuming art. The warp is made of a type of handmade plant-fiber paper, called washi, that is lacquered with gold or silver before it is cut into thin threads; and the weft is fine silk. The process is intensive, but the results are beautiful.

I had considered how to hook to make it look like the weaving. I used the reverse hooking technique that I learned when I lived in New York from 1989 to 1994 with my family. That is where I first encountered rug hooking and became a McGown Certified Instructor.

Reverse hooking means that you make the loops on the wrong side of the backing. That leaves flat, tape-like wool strips on the right side. Normally, I use this technique to make a section of my rug different from the regular loops showing up on the surface. For example, I might do reverse hooking for the background to make the foreground with regular loops more prominent.

To make the mat look like the Saga Nishiki weaving, I did reverse hooking with two or three different colored wools under the backing along a line, and that achieved the effect I was looking for. It was rather difficult to manage those wools, so it took some time to complete. You must count the backing hole numbers with care.

—Chizuko Hayami

This pattern is based on a traditional weaving technique called Rose Path. Saga Nishiki weaving by Michael Cook.

Saga Nishiki weaving by Mihoko Karaki

Saga Nishiki warp is made of specially prepared paper coated with metal leaf. The highest quality warp is made from gold, silver, or platinum; student grades are made of various less-expensive alloys.

The tightly twisted 3-ply silk weft thread for Saga Nishiki comes in varying sizes, wrapped on cards.

Pro Tip

Look at the back of your hooking. If you have hooked along a straight line, you will see what reverse hooking looks like. That is what Chizuko did: she hooked along a straight line from the other side of her foundation cloth.

Saga Nishiki, *8" x 11", reverse hooked with #5-cut on linen. Designed and hooked by Chizuko Hayami, Tokyo, Japan, 2021.*

Weaving | 61

Inspiration: Nejiri-Ume

I live in Tokyo, Japan, and am a member of Chizuko Rug Hooking Studio there. I taught a one-day workshop about creative stitches and developed this original pattern for that workshop. I made a simple design with several types of creative stitches that can be taught in a day. At the lesson, I taught six or seven types of creative stitches using only a large flower. Readers can learn more about creative stitches in Special Effects Using Creative Stitches, by Ingrid Hieronimus, which is the book I used as a reference. I was not thinking that the stitches look like weaving, but I can see that they do.

—Kyoko Okamura

Nejiri-Umi symbol, Mayumi Okamura, Project Japan

Author's Note

I am a weaver. When I saw this beautiful piece online, I was immediately drawn to it because each section looks like it is woven. Parts of the flower look like houndstooth, log cabin, or checks. The background is the reverse-hooking technique that resembles basketweave. Kyoko said she made the background in that style to allow the flower to stand out and look three-dimensional.

Plum blossoms

Nejiri-Ume, *15" x 17", #5-cut wool on linen.*
Designed and hooked using creative stitches by Kyoko Okamura, Tokyo, Japan, 2019.

Inspiration: Tapestry

Why does a design grab your eye? For me, it will probably be a design I've never seen before, or at least with colors I would never have considered. If the colors are already on it, I will try not to see them. Colors, like words, can get stuck in your mind, making it difficult to imagine anything different. And if I did not create the design, then colors and textures are all I can use to make it mine.

I often research my favorite artists or scroll online for antique designs to get inspiration. When I saw the sketch for a tapestry drawn by Marguerite Zorach, the mother of another artist I admire, Dahlov Ipcar, I was fascinated. A few years before I discovered the Zorach sketch, Dahlov and her family had given me permission to reproduce one of her designs, so I already had the contact I needed to ask permission again from the same family.

When they gave permission, all I had to do was resize the sketch in my Rapid Resizer software. The image online was approximately 1" wide, but the software enlarged it to 49" wide by 19½" tall.

Tapestries will show you a whole new world of designs. Look for them in the western European countries where they were most prevalent.

—Liz Gordon

Tapestry sketch by © Marguerite Zorach (1887–1968). Photo shared with permission from family.

Small Animals, *19" x 49", #8-cut wool, sari silks, and yarns on linen. Adapted with permission and hooked by Liz Gordon, Lexington, Virginia, 2019.*

5 Needlework

An invisible thread connects those who are destined to meet, regardless of time, place, and circumstance. The thread may stretch and tangle. But it will never break.

— *Proverb*

In eighteenth-century America, each girl was taught the skills she would need to manage a household and raise a family. Her future work would include making clothing and household linens; therefore, needlework was an essential skill. When she was five or six, she would make her "marking sampler" that would teach her embroidery techniques as well as her letters and numbers. Subsequent samplers made from her childhood until her young womanhood would include more decorative pictures showing advancing proficiency. These beautiful works of art were usually framed and displayed in the parlor for potential suitors to admire. They often included verses about the importance of education, religion, and virtue. Most samplers included a stitched name or initials and the date of completion, making these textiles a record of family history.

Quilting, appliqué, and even knitting might be called needlework, but in this book, we will use the term to refer to those needle arts where the stitches are visible and add to the overall design. Our examples are embroidery and crewel, but needlepoint and cross-stitch could also influence a hooked rug design.

Antique dresser scarf, maker unknown. Inspiration for the pastel rug on the right.

Inspiration: Dresser Scarf

I was a young child in the 1950s, in a home furnished with a lot of hand-me-downs. Our childhood bedroom chests of drawers each had a dresser scarf, embroidered by someone—a granny? An aunt? I never knew who did the embroidery, but I have always had a soft spot in my heart for these lowly bits of domesticity. To this day, if I see a particularly pretty one in an antique shop or a second-hand store, I will buy it. Do I need it? No. Will I use it on a chest of drawers? No. But there will be a time when it will be just what I need for my needlework creations.

For this rug honoring those dresser scarves, I took it up a notch. Instead of hooking a plain white background around the flowers, as you find on most dresser scarves, I added a subtle background behind the embroidered flowers, as if the needlewoman (I always picture a woman) was sewing on chintz or a floral gingham instead of on plain white cotton. Now this dresser scarf has a lovely companion for the floor in front of the dresser.

—Debra Smith

Dresser Scarf, *33" x 24", #8-cut wool on linen. Designed and hooked by Debra Smith, Landisburg, Pennsylvania, 2020. The crocheted edging is a nod to the dresser scarf. Most of the dresser scarves in my childhood home had lovely crocheted finishes.*

Inspiration: Tea Cozy

Inspiration for this rug is a tea cozy that has been passed down through my family. The dimensions are 14" x 12 ½". Materials are coarse, woven linen with cotton thread embroidery (chain stitch, stem stitch, and a wrapped thread stitch), lined with cotton, and the filling may be cotton batting.

Finns love the outdoors and nature, and this love is depicted in their art, be it modern, minimalistic, or steeped in traditional folk handiwork. Trees, flowers, animals, snow, and ice are motifs seen in Finnish artwork.

My family tree from Finland contains textile creators and rug makers, although not specifically rug hookers. My relatives wove rugs on looms and created ryijy (rya) rugs, which are made on a handwoven foundation cloth with knotted wool-yarn pieces.

In her youth, my grandmother attended a women's vocational school that emphasized home economics. Besides the skills she would need to run a successful household, she learned textile arts such as the processing and weaving of linen cloth, embroidery, and sewing. Her graduation certificate shows that she excelled in these areas, and she had planned on becoming a sewing instructor. However, after emigrating to America and raising a family, her focus changed, and she never followed through with her dream vocation.

The tea cozy was found packed in a box along with other family heirlooms after my parents passed away, so there is no longer anyone who would know any specific information about it. It could have been made by my grandmother, or perhaps by one of her sisters or another family member and sent to her as a gift. I know that it must have held special sentimental memories as it appears to have been rarely used.

I was inspired by the simplicity of the two-tone color scheme and by the wrapped-thread embroidery in the center of the flowers, which added texture and interest to the design. I chose a salmon and light-peach checked wool for the background, and three other textured wools that were in the same color family. I designed and added three small birds. I mimicked the embroidery by hooking with an off-white texture, using #5- and #6-cut strips to outline and enhance all the objects. To create the texture in the middle of the flowers, I hooked the beading-stitch in a #8.5 cut, alternating the colors in a checkerboard fashion. I also extended the beading stitch technique out to one of the border rows for continuity. The outermost row of my mat was hooked with a darker, terra cotta plaid, and then the edges were crocheted with #8 strips of terra cotta wool. The crochet edge gave it a rustic, folk-art feel.

—Kris Miller

The tea cozy that inspired the design of the rug

Ready for some Finnish tea

Lovely Day, *23" x 23", #5-, 6-, 8-, and 8.5-cut wool on linen. Designed and hooked by Kris Miller, Howell, Michigan, 2020.*

Inspiration: Wooden Embroidery Blocks

My great-grandmother Philena Moxley (1844–1937) was an entrepreneur and a woman ahead of her time. She spent her early childhood on a farm in Williamstown, Vermont, but when her parents divorced in 1854, Philena and her mother and younger sister moved to Lowell, Massachusetts, to find work.

During the mid-1800s, Lowell was a thriving center for textile production and trade. Throughout her teenage years, Philena worked in a dry goods store, one of the few places a Victorian woman could find honest employment other than the textile mills. She sold fabric and learned the technique of stamping embroidery patterns. In 1865, at age 20, Philena purchased 500 stamping blocks and opened her own store in Lowell.

Fabric at that time was woven in solid colors, so homemade clothing was quite plain. To brighten their wardrobes, ladies embroidered designs on their dresses, coats, and shawls. Philena's stamping blocks provided the actual pattern or guide for the embroidery stitches.

Each block was handmade by soaking a piece of wood in water to soften it so that thin metal strips could easily be tapped into the surface to create shapes such as flowers, leaves, or geometric forms. As the block dried, the wood shrank and anchored the metal strips in place. Most of the blocks were approximately 4" x 8", although some were much larger and were used for rug designs. To create a pattern, the block was dipped into a solution of water and bluing (a cleaning compound), placed on the fabric, and gently tapped with a wooden mallet. When the block was lifted, a blue design remained.

Before closing her dry goods store in the early 1880s, Philena had created over 2,000 individual stamping blocks. The blocks remained in storage until the coal strikes of the 1890s when, unfortunately, many of the larger blocks were burned for warmth. Those that survived—approximately 500—were placed in storage until 1930, when Philena brought them out for a historical demonstration on the stamping process. It is interesting to note that during this demonstration, Philena created a pattern for a hooked rug. She presented the finished rug to the Wenham Museum in Wenham, Massachusetts, the town where she lived with her daughter, Minnie Ashworth. Some of the blocks remained with the Ashworth family and some were donated to the Wenham Historical Society, where they were again placed in storage until 1992, when I started using them to create designs for rug hooking.

These rugs were all hooked based on my great-grandmother's embroidery blocks. My daughter, Lindsay, and I are honored to carry on this legacy.

—Stephanie Allen-Krauss

Antique Stamping Blocks

Philena's wooden stamping blocks. From the collection of Stephanie Allen-Krauss. Photos by Stephanie Allen-Krauss.

Philena Moxley's wooden stamping block, 4" x 6".

Another of Philena's stamping blocks.

This photo shows how the stamp looks when printed on a paper towel.

Moxley Sampler, *14" x 18", #4-cut wool strips on rug warp.*
Designed and hooked by Stephanie Allen-Krauss, Montpelier, Vermont, 2011.

Jesse's Arbor Runner, *14" x 24", #4-cut wool strips on rug warp.
Designed and hooked by Stephanie Allen-Krauss, Montpelier, Vermont, 2006.*

Jesse's Arbor Pillow Square, *14" x 14", #4-cut wool strips on rug warp. Designed and hooked by Stephanie Allen-Krauss, Montpelier, Vermont, 2004.*

Inspiration: Embroidery

I wanted to make a quick stitchery project one Halloween, so I sketched a warty goblin pumpkin based on one I'd grown in my garden, and then I made some tissue-paper ghosts and stuck them on the window for inspiration. I liked the simplicity of the embroidered piece, including the embroidered ghosts, so I framed it and now I hang it up each fall.

I decided to make a companion rug, so I drew it on some linen and got to work. I love the moody sky and the way the ghosts are floating in the air. I plan to hang them both at Halloween each year. I finished this rug with binding tape.

—Lin Keller

Halloween embroidery designed and stitched by Lin Keller, Shermans Dale, Pennsylvania, 2020.

On Halloween, *16" x 16", #8- and 8.5-cut hand-dyed wool strips on linen. Designed and hooked by Lin Keller, Shermans Dale, Pennsylvania, 2021.*

Inspiration: Samplers

Samplers. The word evokes a vision of a past era of charm, elegance, and gentle work. Samplers are personal and are a diary of the maker's developing needlework skills. They often include some letters or an entire alphabet, numbers, and, sometimes, a phrase or prayer. Some incorporate the name of the maker (often a schoolgirl), ages, dates, the name of a teacher or a location. Most were produced by women and girls, according to the Smithsonian Institution's Museum of American History and, consequently, offer great insight into the lives of women and girls throughout history.

While searching for inspiration, I found the sampler collection of the Metropolitan Museum of Art in New York City. The museum's collection is extensive and includes thousands of examples, and most can be found in an online resource that includes images and historical information.

Two of my favorite examples are separated by centuries and culture. The first is Flemish and dated 1698. According to the museum, it is thought to have originated in Friesland, in the northwest of the Netherlands. It is linen and silk thread on linen and measures 25¼" by 9¼". Samplers of this type are characterized chiefly by alphabets and tree-of-life motifs. This sampler also features pierced and crowned hearts, checkerboards, and motifs of brides and grooms. The letters VM are most likely the initials of the sampler's maker. The dates 1667, 1692, 1697, and 1698 seen below the images might commemorate births or marriages of family members.

Another of my favorites is an American Shaker sampler stitched by Mariah Boil, who was born in 1832 and stitched her sampler in 1844 (at age 12) in Pleasant Hill, Kentucky. It is stitched with silk and cotton on a linen and cotton material. The sampler measures 13" x 11¾". According to the museum, this sampler is quite unusual as few samplers were made in Shaker communities.

—Ellen Banker

Embroidered Sampler, *25¼" x 9¼", embroidered linen and silk on linen. From the collection of Mrs. Lathrop Colgate Harper. Photo courtesy of the Metropolitan Museum of Art, New York, New York, Open Access, public domain.*

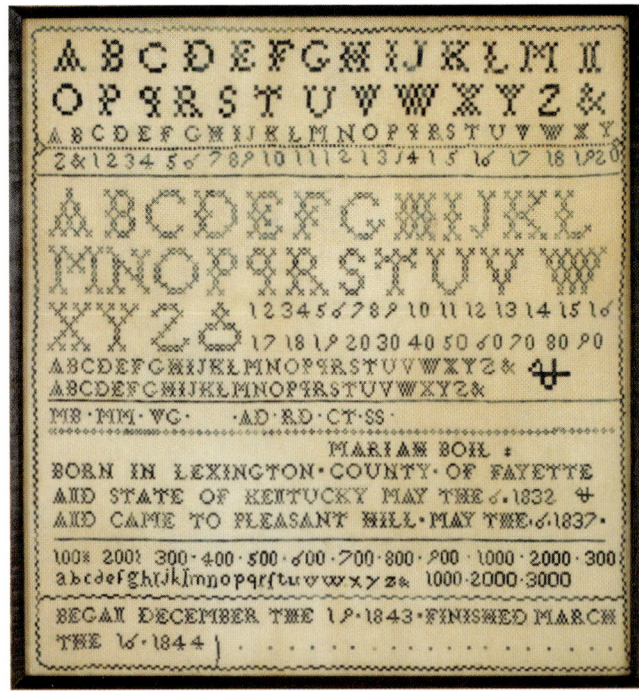

Shaker Sampler, *13" x 11¾", silk and cotton embroidery on linen/cotton. Photo courtesy of the Metropolitan Museum of Art, New York, New York, Open Access, public domain.*

A Rug Hooker's Sampler, *20" x 40", #4-, 6- and 8-cut dyed and recycled wool on linen. Designed and hooked by Ellen Banker, Williamsburg, Virginia, 2017. Hooking each letter in an entirely different style was like finishing a little mini rug 26 times.*

LYNN BOHANNON

Needlework | 77

The Carrot Sampler Number 10, 20" x 40", #4-, 6- and 8-cut dyed wool on linen. Designed and hooked by Ellen Banker, Williamsburg, Virginia, 2018. *The Carrot Sampler* might be my favorite sampler of all my designs. I think its simplicity gives it an understated feeling, even an elegance, for such a large rug.

Sampler Number 22, 20" x 20", #4-, 6- and 8-cut dyed wool on linen. Designed and hooked by Ellen Banker, Williamsburg, Virginia, 2018. I think of my designs as "suggestions" and hope that people will add or subtract elements as they wish. The original pattern for this sampler was designed for a class. It was intended to be a simple yet elegant design, with an emphasis on the background and the bunny!

Autumn Sampler, 20" x 40", #4-, 6- and 8-cut dyed and recycled wool on linen. Designed and hooked by Ellen Banker, Williamsburg, Virginia, 2021. I love the colors of the fall. This sampler was designed especially for autumn with its brisk winds, falling leaves, and yummy pumpkins. On our farm in Vermont, we grew pumpkins of lots of different colors—except orange. The sampler's green pumpkin is a celebration of our farm.

Inspiration: Polish Folk Art from the Lowicz Region

As the firstborn to Polish immigrant parents, my life has been steeped in Polish culture and heritage. My first language was Polish, and I didn't learn English until I went to nursery school at age four. I distinctly remember practicing my first word in English, "hello," while holding my father's hand as he walked with me to meet the teacher. I grew up surrounded by everything Polish, which included traditional Polish folk art. Most of that art derived from the Lowicz region in central Poland, where my family is from, or from the Carpathian Mountains, on the southern border of the country. In my home there were Polish textiles, folk costumes, houseware items, artwork hanging on the wall, and greeting cards. Many of the motifs originated from cut-paper patterns and similarly embroidered motifs on fabric. When I first started rug hooking, I wanted to hook a rug showcasing this type of traditional folk art.

A few years ago, a friend of mine gave me a pillow that had a Lowicz folk-art flower pattern. The sawtooth design in the border is also traditional. There is a clear symmetry in the pattern that derives from its origins as cut-paper patterns.

A hallmark of the Lowicz region's folk art is bright colors. The background is almost always all white, and the sawtooth pattern along the border is traditionally black. Occasionally these are reversed, with a black background and white border, but rarely do these patterns diverge from the contrasting black-and-white theme.

I worked on the design to ensure that it would represent the culture. I chose colors that are seen most frequently in this type of folk art: vivid reds, blues, greens, and bright yellows.

This pattern features one central flower flanked by two pairs of flowers. In keeping with the traditional symmetry, the flowers surrounding the central floral motif would mirror each other across a central vertical line, so I had to plan three different color schemes for each of those motifs. Each of the floral design elements contains multiple layers, so I assembled the color plan for each flower, starting with the largest, back layer first. I decided that the largest layer of the central flower would be red, that of the next pair of flowers would be orange, and that of the final pair of flowers would be dark blue. Decisions for the remainder of the colors in each flower flow from those initial color decisions. Since the inspiration for the rug is traditionally built via paper cutting, background colors frequently come through the layers. Translating this paper-cut effect into a rug design, for example, you can see that in the central flower, the smallest blue layer has "cut outs" through which the orange layer can be seen.

Being a resident of the twenty-first century, I leveraged artistic license to give this project a modern feel with the use of the fluorescent green. Centuries ago, that color wasn't available, although it can be found in the color palette that has begun to appear in modern folk-art pieces.

The background was a challenge. Embroidered folk costumes from the Carpathian Mountains are traditionally sewn onto felted wool, and I wanted to imitate that effect. I couldn't use straight-off-the-bolt white or natural wool because the contrast would be too stark. Instead, I hand-dyed the background wool with a very light-yellow wash to give it a more natural felted wool look. When hooking the background, I used meandered hooking and avoided too much echoing, using instead directional hooking to try to emulate the look of felted wool.

Finally, achieving a crisp sawtooth required deliberate hooking techniques. I wanted the black sawtooth pointing toward the central motif, with clearly defined, consistent points. This rug is large and drawing the pattern with that many straight edges on the border was difficult, with the linen sometimes stretching unpredictably, even before distorting the shape with hooking. I nearly opted out of this design element in anticipation of much frustration. However, in the end, I learned how to make straight edges out of inherently non-straight materials. I did rework parts of the border to ensure that it was tight and balanced, especially at the corners.

When I showed this rug to family members back in Poland, they immediately recognized the local folk-art origins. Now I get to relive my fondest childhood memories through this piece. I've already thought about how nice it will be to pass it on to my children—fortunately, they seem to like the rug as well.

—Ania Knap

Printed pillow cover with Lowicz folk-art flower motifs

Polish Folk Art from the Lowicz Region, *35" x 41", #4- and 6-cut wool on linen. Designed by Monique Frechette and hooked by Ania Knap, Reading, Massachusetts, 2021.*

Inspiration: Embroidery

The idea that one medium can and does influence another is nothing new. We are all bombarded by a huge variety of visual stimuli every day and we naturally respond to this in our own work. But for this project, I intended to be specific in my starting point and intentional in producing a rug from my research.

I narrowed my influences down to sixteenth- and seventeenth-century embroidery, initially thinking about English samplers. I knew that these early textiles would provide a rich stream of inspiration. Although my early ideas were based on samplers, I was excited to come across some petit-point needlework slips from Traquair House in Scotland. These had been in storage for centuries, preserved and protected from light damage. The colors were rich and the designs beautiful. I also came across a an embroidered textile of The Tree of Life from the first half of the seventeenth century. It depicts many types of fruits, as referenced in the book of Revelation, with additional images of vegetables and animals. The embroidery is on canvas and is worked with silk threads in tent, gobelin, and couching stitches. It is in the collection of The Metropolitan Museum of Art and is in the public domain.

Not wanting to produce just a copy I played around with different elements from both the slips and the tapestry. I generated many thumbnail sketches to try out different arrangements. I changed the scale, the colors, and mirroring or repeating various images. This approach automatically creates a completely new design. I eventually decided to use the swans from The Tree of Life textile as the main image. I increased the scale and added a mirror image of the swan. I didn't slavishly copy the original, rather I took the slightly-angular swan and simply drew it larger. I wasn't concerned about making an exact copy; I merely used it as a source. Often just changing an image from one textile source into another will automatically create some differences. Rug hooking with ¼" strips of wool automatically limits the detail you can achieve, in contrast to tiny stitches on canvas or silk from the originals.

I focused the eye on the central image by using a dark blue on the outside edges and lighter hues as I moved in toward the swans. To frame the swans, I isolated certain flowers and leaves from the Traquair petit point and incorporated them in the design. I intentionally kept it very simple, repeating the same elements in slightly different sizes and angles. This contrasts with the original source pieces, both of which are very detailed. I chose bright colors for the leaves and flowers, with a darker background made up of five or six different teal wools.

This was an interesting project, and I recommend researching specific sources for inspiration and information. Start with an era and a region of the world that interests you and go from here.

—Joanne Page

Sketches showing elements from petit point slips

The Tree of Life, 22½" x 24", *British silk thread embroidery on canvas. Unknown maker from the first half of the seventeenth century. Photo courtesy of the Metropolitan Museum of Art, New York, New York, Open Access, public domain.*

Color selection

Ready to put on the linen

Feathered Friends, *36" x 25", #8-cut wool on linen.
Designed and hooked by Joanne Page, Wake Forest, North Carolina, 2011.*

Inspiration: Crewel Embroidery

While looking for new rug hooking techniques and styles, I was drawn to the detail, bright colors, whimsical flowers, and animals in Jacobean embroidery. The playfulness of this style is accentuated by different stitching techniques, such as French knots, cable, chain, and rope stitch.

As England increased its trade in the East Indies, more vibrant dyes were brought back to England and used in needlework. In Jacobean crewel embroidery, wool yarn is used, providing a more textured look. Rug hooking as a medium is beautiful for the Jacobean embroidery style. Since this particular Tree of Life pattern did not have any animals, I added a small squirrel.

There are many resources that are not under copyright that you can use to create your own design by combining various motifs or hooking a single motif. There are also resources to learn how to hook creative stiches that mimic the different stitching techniques seen in Jacobean embroidery crewel. I hooked this pattern using a mix of 6-value swatches and spot dyes cut into #3 size strips.

—Elaine Montambeau

Crewel Work 7, *from* Book of Patterns and Instructions for American Needlework.
Wool crewel yarn embroidered on wool upholstery fabric.
Created by Ruth Orvis, Syracuse, New York.

Author's Note

Jacobean crewel embroidery is so named because it was popular in the early seventeenth century, when King James I ruled England. (It is called Jacobean because the Latin form of James is Jacob.) Similar embroidery was also found during the reign of his predecessor, Queen Elizabeth I. It was usually done using fanciful stitches with 2-ply wool yarn on linen. I love Elaine's use of shading to make this stunning rug look so similar to its embroidered inspiration. However, you could also just outline the shapes and fill them in for a more primitive look. Or you could do both a shaded and simpler version. What about a monochromatic look with whites, grays, and blacks? So many possibilities . . .

Jacobean Crewel. *Adapted from a Jacobean crewel handbag pattern by Pearl K. McGown. 13" x 13", #3-cut wool on linen, including 6-value swatches and spot dyes. Designed by Pearl K. McGown and hooked by Elaine Montambeau, 2021.*

Inspiration: Redwork

Redwork became popular between 1855 and 1925. The name applies to outline embroidery, usually stitched with colorfast Turkey red cotton floss. Preprinted linen dishcloths and quilt blocks were widely available to the needleworker.

This vintage linen dishcloth was stitched by my grandmother. I placed it on a light box to copy the pattern. The simple yet elegant design translated easily into rug hooking, but it's important to note that I did not add all the details and I eliminated some of the lines. Often in rug hooking, less is more. In this case, the extra lines would only confuse the eye of the viewer. I hooked the mat with a #5 cut for the outline and a #7 cut for the background. The color, or lack of it, allows the design to stand out. The mat was finished with recycled skirt wool, and I added a sleeve to the back in coordinating wool, for ease of hanging. A simple but beautiful project.

— Nancy Zeppelin Parcels

Linen dishcloth with redwork embroidery

Redwork, *10" x 10", #5- and 7-cut wool on linen.
Designed and hooked by Nancy Zeppelin Parcels, Rustburg, Virginia, 2020.*

Inspiration: Sashiko

Sashiko, which means "little jabs," is a type of Japanese embroidery that is usually done with white cotton thread on indigo fabric. Historically this embroidery was used to repair worn clothing in a beautiful way. Long, cold winters gave families time to make and repair garments. Sashiko stitching was also used to strengthen and reinforce the fabric.

I took a class to learn sashiko embroidery and I absolutely loved everything about it, except that I am so terribly slow. Sashiko is beautiful because of the simplicity of mostly straight lines that make such lovely, geometric patterns. To hook a rug with the look of sashiko, I used narrow strips of wool and the beading stitch to duplicate the embroidery. I can enjoy this rug until I finish my authentic sashiko piece to complement it. I will happily take my time.

—Kathleen Eckhaus

Sashiko jacket, late nineteenth century Japan, indigo-dyed plain-weave cotton, quilted and embroidered with white cotton thread. Photo courtesy of the Metropolitan Museum of Art, New York, New York, Open Access, public domain.

Hand-embroidered sashiko bag

Sashiko, 19" x 19", #6- and 8-cut wool on linen.
Designed and hooked by Kathleen Eckhaus, Elliottsburg, Pennsylvania, 2021.

6 Other Rugs

The soul of the apartment is the carpet.

— Edgar Allan Poe

Rugs come in many varieties, but the ones we are using here were inspired by a Native American rug, an early hooked rug, and the vast variety of Oriental carpets. Early human history shows evidence of shearing sheep and using the wool to make utilitarian items. Rugs kept dirt floors warm, were bedcovers on a winter's night, and sometimes decorated walls. Native American rugs were woven on either tapestry or back-strap looms. Hooked rugs were made of worn wool garments. Asian rugs were often complicated in design and made of tufted yarn, each loop pulled by the maker. There are crocheted, cross-stitched, appliquéd, woven, and braided rugs, too. Any of these could inspire a hooked design. Look at what's under your feet. Can you design a rug?

Design as You Go

Revise, revise, revise! I rarely draw something on linen and hook it just the way I drew it. But it's easy to change your ideas. Here you see that I thought the pansies were too small. So I drew a larger one, cut it out and traced it with different colored marker. It can be hard to figure out which lines are correct—which lines you really want to follow—but changing your drawing is better than forever wishing you had.

When I begin a design on paper, I use pencil so that I can erase and make changes, but once something is drawn on linen with permanent marker, there is no going back. However, if you use a different colored marker, you can fix whatever you like. I have been known to mark an X over an unneeded line or change my mind multiple times, which requires several different-colored markers. You can even write notes to yourself on the linen. All unnecessary lines and comments will be completely covered by your beautiful hooking. Ta-da!

Flowers were too small.

Revised flowers—perfect!

Inspiration: Navajo Weaving

I am very new to the rug-hooking scene: one project done, one in progress, and ideas for yet another. My first project took a little over a year to complete, just because of a lack of time—or should I say, a lack of setting aside time. I do much better when I can join my friends to hook together, and I began my rug-hooking journey shortly before the 2020 pandemic.

I find Native American art especially appealing, partly because of their connection to nature and because of their beautiful craftmanship. The decision to make a Navajo-design hooked rug was the easy part. I had an example of a real Navajo rug that was my inspiration for a design. I knew some of the design had to be changed because I'm just learning and felt there were things I could not easily do. I had to use my imagination.

When choosing my colors, I looked at many examples of real Navajo rugs for inspiration. I learned that color choices have great meaning in Navajo art, and though I don't know all those meanings, the colors contain both cultural and spiritual importance and connect the past, present, and future for Navajo people.

The red wool that was given to me for this project by a friend was from a blanket that her dad gave to her before he passed. Now my rug has a past, present, and future connection, too.

I underestimated how much wool I needed of each color, but my friends taught me how to blend in different values of the same color. I learned it's okay to have variations, and I believe it made my rug look even better.

I really like the flexibility of rug hooking. If something doesn't work one way, there are other ways to do it. I now have a rug that I love and that will be a treasured heirloom for generations to come.

—Rachel Lea Olendorf Beaston

Miniature woven Navajo rug, 5" x 7". Purchased from the weaver in 2019.

Author's Note

Navajo rugs and blankets are woven on either an upright or on a back-strap loom. They traditionally don't leave fringe. In the seventeenth century, Spanish explorers brought Iberian Churra sheep, which have been bred to what is now the Navajo Churro breed. This wool is excellent for rugs and blankets.

Pro Tip

To eliminate the influence of color as you are designing and color planning,, take a photo of your inspiration with your phone and change it to black-and-white. After you have hooked your rug, you can take another black-and-white photo to see if any of your colors are too close in value. An easy remedy is just to do a bit of outlining to solve the problem spots.

Wilder Spirits, *26" x 40", #8-cut wool on linen. Inspired by Navajo weavings, and hooked by Rachel Beaston, Blain, Pennsylvania, 2022.*

Inspiration: Oriental Rugs

These are two examples of Oriental hooked rugs, both designed by Edward Sands Frost, who was a tin peddler turned hooked-rug pattern maker from 1867 to 1870. Many of his original tin patterns have been acquired by Greenfield Village and the Henry Ford Museum in Dearborn, Michigan. The patterns are available through W. Cushing & Co.

Hooking an Oriental can be quite the relaxing journey. There is an old hooking phrase: You work on a floral and rest on an Oriental. This means shading flowers can be tedious, as there are many value changes throughout the flower itself, but when one hooks an Oriental, after one-quarter of the rug is planned out, then it's just a matter of pulling loops. There are also the classic Oriental colors which one can choose from, making color planning easier. When hooking an Oriental, it is common practice to keep the background and as many elements as possible hooked linearly across the rug, to mimic the back-and-forth of a woven rug.

The *Large Frost Oriental* gave me some places to put personal hidden messages. One corner has a smiley face, one corner a pumpkin, one corner my initials; it also has my age when I hooked it and is dated in Roman numerals. There is also some antique wool paisley in the rug, as a tribute to my mentor.

On the *Small Frost Oriental*, I designed and added the outer zigzag and dashed border, which grounds the rug. There are also several playful things hidden in this rug. One corner has the date in Roman numerals, one corner has a COVID bubble, and one has a heart for hope and love. I also worked my initials into the border.

Designing an Oriental on your own can be challenging and fun. There are many reference books that explain the meaning of the design elements and have historic reference as to color and style. Take some time and care to make your rugs tell a story. Often the viewer never notices the details you've added unless you point them out. Find clever ways to subtly make the rug your very own. Remember it's your rug, your art, your journey.

— Nancy Zeppelin Parcels

Small Frost Oriental, *24" x 45", #3- and 7-cut on linen. Designed by Edward Sands Frost and hooked by Nancy Zeppelin Parcels, Rustburg, Virginia.*

94 | Hooked on Handwork

Author's Note

The variations in background color in these rugs were intentional and are called abrash, a word that comes from the Turkish word for mottled. This occurred because the dyes used by nomadic weavers changed according to the landscape, dye lots, and yarn variations. Nancy intentionally added them to her hooked pieces. The term *Oriental rug* describes carpets from Morocco, North Africa, the Middle East, Central Asia, and northern India, an area sometimes called the rug belt. Patterns are followed to make the intricate designs. Finally, the tufts on the top of the rug are trimmed evenly to make a soft pile.

Large Frost Oriental, *37" x 73". Designed by Edward Sands Frost and hooked by Nancy Zeppelin Parcels, Rustburg, Virginia.*

Inspiration: The World Around You

Magdalena Briner Eby is a woman who inspired countless rug hookers. As a rug hooker living in Perry County, Pennsylvania, I am well aware of the legacy of Magdalena Briner Eby, who lived her entire life in this county, from 1832 until 1915.

After becoming a widow only two years into her marriage, she devoted her life to caring for family members. She did a wide variety of chores both outside and inside the home, which included quilting and rug hooking, using and repurposing worn-out clothing into folk-art pieces to beautify the home. Her hooked rugs are sought after today as prime examples of American folk art.

Ten years ago, a few of us rug hookers collaborated to form a group to meet and share our love of this fiber art. We named our group Magdalena Rug Hookers out of respect and love for this woman, who made Perry County her home for 83 years.

In 2020, to celebrate its bicentennial, Perry County installed historical markers to honor local people who left their mark on the county. Rug Hooking Traditions along with the authors of the book on Magdalena (Kathy Wright and Evelyn Lawrence) launched a fundraiser for a historic marker to honor Magdalena. Our group hooked a special rug to be raffled off to raise the necessary funds.

The pattern we hooked, *Magdalena's Farm*, was generously donated by Barb Carroll of The Woolley Fox. This pattern was passed around within our group, each member hooking a motif, resulting in a beautiful rug that was successfully raffled off.

Magdalena didn't have fancy tools to work with and most likely never had an art class, but she joyfully hooked whimsical motifs on her rugs. Countless rug hookers worldwide have been inspired by this country woman, who lived a simple life in our rural county. There are Facebook groups of admirers and many new rugs designed in a Magdalena Briner Eby style. For someone who probably didn't think she was an artist, she certainly made her mark in the world of fiber arts.

—Karen Larsen

Great Granddaughter's Rug, 43½" x 32½", mixed fibers on burlap or linen. Designed and hooked by Magdalena Briner Eby, Perry County, Pennsylvania, ca. 1880. Photo courtesy of Rug Hooking Traditions, Oxford, Ohio.

Magdalena's Farm, 37½" x 25", #8-cut recycled and new wool on linen. Pattern donated by Barb Carroll of The Woolley Fox. Hooked by members of the Magdalena Rug Hookers of Perry County, Pennsylvania, 2019.

KATHLEEN ECKHAUS

Other Rugs | 97

7 Fabric Prints

One should either be a work of art, or wear a work of art.

— Oscar Wilde

If you need inspiration for a rug design, look to your local fabric store. Fanciful flowers, amazing geometrics, and border ideas are all there to get your creative juices flowing. You might see some cute animals or trains and cars on children's fabrics. Get ideas for motifs and color combinations, too. Avoid the licensed fabrics because the images on those are copyrighted.

Inspiration: Paisley Fabric

Paisley designs and vintage wool paisley shawls have inspired many rug hookers. The timeless designs flow and always give us a reliable color palette. Damaged shawls are often cut into 1" strips and used to hook rugs. The design on this handbag was inspired by a paisley shawl.

There are many patterns for making handbags, pouches, and purses, and the needed hardware can be found at most fabric stores.

— Nancy Zeppelin Parcels

The back of the purse

Author's Note

Experts still debate the origin of the paisley motif, which is described as a teardrop shape, but it is believed to have come from Iran or India in the eighteenth or nineteenth century. The British East India company brought Kashmir shawls to the United Kingdom, where fabric bearing this shape was woven in Paisley, a town in Scotland that was the center for textile production at the time. The fabric woven there was cheaper than any that was imported, so the Scottish paisley became a fashion accessory for all walks of life. In the 1960s, paisley prints had a resurgence in popularity helped along by The Beatles—in their Eastern-influenced phase, the band members often wore paisley-adorned garments and John Lennon even had a paisley Rolls-Royce. Paisley designs were part of the bandanas of cowboys and bikers.

Paisley Purse, *14" x 12", multiple cuts of wool and fabric from vintage paisley shawl hooked on linen foundation. Designed and hooked by Nancy Zeppelin Parcels, Rustburg, Virginia, 2010. This photo shows the front of the purse with the paisley shawls in the background.*

Inspiration: Paisley Fabric

In 2014, my daughter and I thought it would be fun to work together on a creative adventure. I had been rug hooking since 2007 and thought combining her drawing skills and my hooking would be fun. To my delight, she agreed, and we began to brainstorm. She wanted to play with paisleys, and since I have long been a fan of them, we were on our way. She fueled her creative fires with favorite patterns from our own wardrobes.

One was a large scarf with a bold, colorful pattern highlighting beautiful paisleys. We both loved the patterns within these paisleys but knew that much detail would be difficult to hook. Instead, she took inspiration from the idea of layering patterns within the paisleys and incorporated that idea in her design.

Paisley Rain Forest, 18" x 18", #3-cut wool on linen.
Designed by Monique Frechette and hooked by Ania Knap, Reading, Massachusetts, 2014.

Paisley silk shawl, Ania's first career wardrobe purchase

Paisley cotton-print blouse, a favorite from the artist's high school days

There were many other natural elements around her that formed the creative vision that became the final product. The wonder of artistic inspiration is the unique perspective of each individual, taking in the beauty of her surroundings to inspire new creations. I hope that readers of this book will take that lesson away from this rug—something as simple as your favorite scarf can help you create a rug to be proud of.

Given the complexity of the pattern and its size, I knew it would be hooked in a #3 cut. I'm a fan of bright colors, but I was specifically inspired by Lilly Pulitzer's signature colors—bright pinks and greens.

The most important aspect of the color planning was the color placement for the three central motifs. Focusing first on figuring out the two paisleys and one leaf, I could repeat those colors in the other elements. By doing so, the colors used in those central elements can be seen across imaginary diagonal lines throughout the rug. This helps the eye move smoothly over the piece.

I finished *Paisley Rain Forest* by using leftover 8-value swatches to create a binding strip for the rug. Similar to the method that one would use to bind a quilt, I used the multicolor pieced-wool strip to finish the piece. This method of finishing allowed me to use the same colors that are in the rug to give it a frame that continued the visual theme, while also providing a border to complete the rug.

—Ania Knap

Author's Note

Lilly Pulitzer and her husband owned several orange groves in Florida. She set up a stand to sell fresh orange juice and ended up with juice all over her clothing. To solve the problem, she made a sleeveless dress of brightly colored fabric—and her customers raved about it. When her dresses were selling more than her juice, she knew she'd discovered her calling and founded a hugely successful design company. If her name is not familiar to you, do an internet search to see the colors she is known for today.

Inspiration: Contemporary Fabric

The fabric that inspired this mat is bright and cheerful with clean modern lines. I liked the colors of the flowers and decided to use the same color family. I used wool from my stash. Instead of using swatches for shading, I chose wool with greater differences in intensity to give definition to the flower petals. Using the same wool in each flower and bud unifies the design. Although the background of the inspiration piece is lovely, I decided that a neutral background would be more effective in showcasing the flowers. I used a variety of off-white, tan, and ecru wools, adding a coordinating green for interest.

Rather than following the outline of the flowers throughout the background, I added curved lines and followed them as well. The background was not entirely hit-or-miss; decisions were made about which colors to use next. Using the green from the flower stems for initials and date helped to blend them into the design.

I drew the design freehand on the linen. My goal was never to have an exact copy, but rather to capture the general feeling of the inspiration fabric.

—Gloria McPherson

Printed cotton fabric. Gloria used a portion about 12" x 12" as her inspiration for her hooked piece.

Vibrant, 13¼" x 13", #8-cut wool on linen. Designed and hooked by Gloria McPherson, New Bloomfield, Pennsylvania, 2021.

Inspiration: African Fabric

I based the design for this rug on fabric that I brought back from Tanzania. African fabric is known for vibrancy and bright colors, but brown is my favorite color (think coffee, chocolate, garden soil), so I was naturally drawn to this piece. When I looked more closely at the pattern, I realized that these sets of circles would be easy to transfer into a colorful rug design. I used drinking glasses to make the circles. Some of my rug-hooking friends told me that if I really wanted a bright rug, I should avoid earth tones and anything muted. This was very much outside my comfort zone, but I managed to hook with colors. Even the background, although quiet and subdued, is not brown!

I also decided not to plan too much—not to have reasons for my color choices—but just to hook and aim for whimsy. I live in the county where Magdalena Briner Eby lived and hooked her well-known primitive rugs. Her designs do not seem to be planned. One motif in many of her rugs is a tree with circles that is sometimes referred to as a lollipop tree. But no one knows for sure.

Have you wondered about the reasons for design elements in the rugs of other artists? I have.

It's natural to try to understand choices or imagine yourself in the rug maker's shoes. Well, in my rug, the circles aren't penny candy any more than Magdalena's trees are sporting lollipops. Maybe those who see this rug will wonder why I chose the colors that I did, why I spaced my circle groupings the way I did, or why I added the sprinkles in the background. I'll never tell. As they say, art is in the eye of the beholder and the maker. That is enough.

—Kathleen Eckhaus

Creative Tip

Other sources of design inspiration are wallpaper and gift wrap. Sometimes one motif can be the basis of an entire rug pattern.

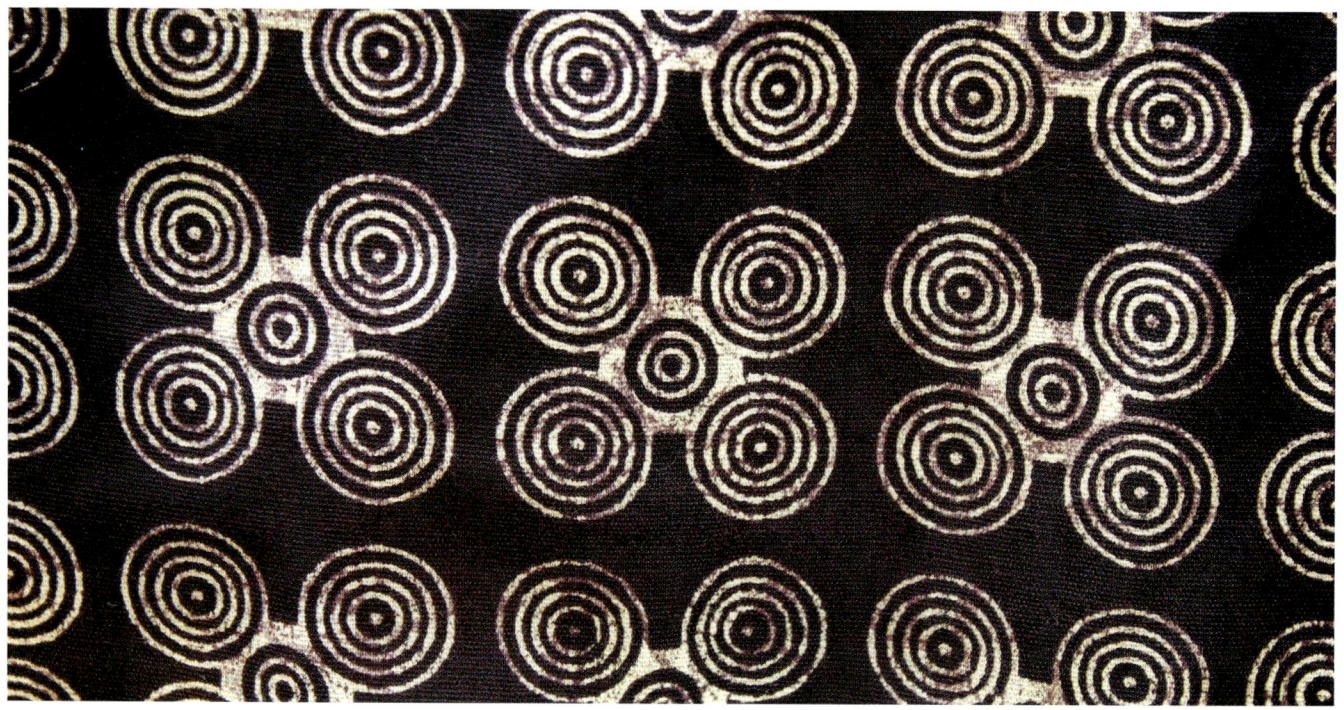

Printed cotton fabric from Tanzania

Penny Candy, *21" x 24", #8-cut wool on linen. Designed and hooked by Kathleen Eckhaus, Elliottsburg, Pennsylvania, 2020.*

Fabric Prints | 107

8 Other Handcrafts

Art matters because it illustrates the human experience—the wonder of it, the bewilderment of it, the whimsy of it, and so much more. We would not be connected so deeply without the existence of art.
— Kathleen Dinsmore, National Endowment for the Arts

Look at the design on this pitcher. How about the patterns in the furniture? Get inspired by the designs all around you.

Inspiration: Pottery

Acoma Pueblo, often called Sky City, is built on top of a mesa approximately 70 miles west of Albuquerque, New Mexico. The Pueblo has been continually inhabited for more than 2,000 years, and the people of the Pueblo continue to practice the pottery-making traditions of their ancestors. The pottery is made from a slate-like clay found in the surrounding hills.

I was attracted to this Acoma pot because of its soft shape and bold, simple, primitive design. The choice to do a round hooked mat made it possible for me to visually deconstruct the pot to show the whole design at once. My inspiration for doing it this way was remembering world maps I've seen that look like someone took a spherical globe, cut it, and laid it out flat.

To make my design look primitive and less than perfect, I marked one-quarter of the whole circle on paper and then drew each of the elements by hand. I marked my linen backing carefully, with a dot at the center and at each of the cardinal points, so that I could line up my quarter pattern and trace it four times to create the whole circle.

I have an affinity for hooking round mats, and in this case, the shape is suggestive of the object, the round pot. I made the mat large enough to look good on a table or countertop.

The original pot is black and white with a single brown line at the upper edge. I hooked my piece with earth-toned, hand-dyed, and as-is wool strips on unbleached primitive linen.

—Karen Larsen

KATHLEEN ECKHAUS

Shards, *24" diameter, #8-cut wool on linen. Designed and hooked by Karen Larsen, Elliottsburg, Pennsylvania, 2020.*

Handmade pottery from Acoma Pueblo, New Mexico

Inspiration: Stained Glass

Frank Lloyd Wright's designs use simple lines and symmetry. The pattern and color plan for this piece reflect these simple features. You can draw a line down the middle of this pattern, and everything on the left is a mirror image of the right. There are no curves, only straight lines. This pattern was specifically inspired by the window designs at the Lake Geneva Hotel in Lake Geneva, Wisconsin. The windows in the lobby consisted of an upper row of tulip art-glass windows over a lower row of plain art-glass windows. I found a detail photo of the upper row of tulip windows online, which were the inspiration for the hooked piece. The photograph was taken by Richard Nickel in 1967. The hotel was heavily damaged in a fire and subsequently demolished in 1970.

I used shimmer wool to mimic the effect of light shining through a real stained-glass window. This project was a great opportunity to showcase an application for shimmer wool to achieve a non-traditional effect. (I also like this pattern because it resembles an M, the first letter of my eldest daughter's name. It makes me think of her.)

My first decision: the background would be white, like glass. Then, I decided to use three colors: yellow, blue, and green—two primary colors (yellow and blue) and a secondary color (green) that is derived from equal parts of the two primary colors.

Wherever I can, I play symmetry games with colors. In this rug, there is a pattern with the greens and yellows through the middle of the piece. On the left side of the rug, I hooked color 1, color 2, and then color 3. On right side I used the same colors but started with color 2, color 3, and then color 1. Most of the pattern is hooked with shimmer wool, which can be seen in the photos. The iridescence it presents and the visual simplicity are lovely. Despite all the bling, it's very simple.

—Ania Knap

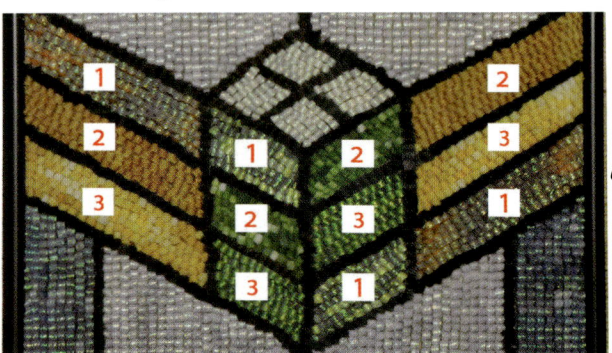

Color symmetry

Frank Lloyd Wright Stained Glass, 10" x 10", #4-cut wool and shimmer wool strips on rug warp. Designed and hooked by Ania Knap, Reading, Massachusetts, 2014.

Inspiration: Floorcloth

My inspiration for this rug was a hand-painted canvas floor cloth by Pamela Steele. The design was taken from the front of a Pennsylvania dower chest that dated to the 1800s. The simplicity in color and design is typical of Pennsylvania Dutch folk art. I designed a rug to go with the floor cloth and use both in my kitchen.

I used golds and yellows from my scraps and noodles to give the flowers depth without using a lot of different colors. The red background was from four Pendleton skirts, all different shades of gray, from light to dark. The skirts were deconstructed and then dyed together in the same red formula. This gives the background movement even though it is one color.

— Nancy Zeppelin Parcels

Author's Note

Floorcloths in colonial days were made from used sailcloth. Designs were painted freehand or with of stencils, and then coated to make them waterproof. Floorcloths were used directly on floors or on top of valuable carpets to keep them clean and free from wear. Today, artists usually make floorcloths on canvas.

Primitive Flower Box, *40" x 28", #6-, 7-, and 8-cut wool on linen. Designed and hooked by Nancy Zeppelin Parcels, Rustburg, Virginia, 2004.*

Hand-painted floor cloth in the Pennsylvania Dutch style by Pamela Steele

Inspiration: Fraktur

Fraktur or sampler? Heinrich Diefenbach (1771–1837), self-described as a fraktur artist/scrivener and minister, created the original 9" x 7" birth certificates of the Spengler children around 1800. Most frakturs originated in Pennsylvania German areas around the eighteenth century and were hand-drawn to illustrate documents celebrating births, deaths, baptisms, weddings, house blessings, and schoolhouse awards. Most samplers were stitched by young schoolgirls in New England. But Diefenbach's fraktur drawings, which were a blend of both arts, were created in Virginia's Shenandoah Valley where I live. Just another fact that piqued my interest.

I found this images on an online antique company auction. Having been a collector of antique samplers and a fraktur lover, I was drawn to the piece, never having seen anything like it before. Diefenbach's designs added whole human figures, not usually seen on frakturs. And the colors in his drawings are more muted than the bright golds, greens, blues, and reds seen on most frakturs.

You'll find hundreds of fraktur and sampler designs online, and the old ones are usually copyright free. One of my wall hangings is a design from a fraktur bookplate I found inside an old book.

—Liz Gordon

Original fraktur, Heinrich Diefenbach.

Margaret Spengler, *18" x 21", #8-cut wool with silk for the hands and for painting the faces. Designed and hooked by Liz Gordon, Lexington, Virginia, 2015.*

Inspiration: Quilling

My best friend, Laura, tackled many different art mediums during the pandemic, including quilling. I left it in her hands about what shape, image, and colors she wanted, and then I would try my best to make a hooked rug to emulate her creation. She decided on a hamsa design, which is widely found in Middle Eastern and Northern African cultures and is a symbol of protection that also represents blessings, power, and strength.

I was hesitant about tackling this project for two reasons: this would be only my second hooked rug, and it was suggested that I make quillies to simulate the quilled paper. This was a "learn as you go" project. I watched videos on YouTube to see how to make quillies, but mostly it was trial and error to figure out how to make the different shapes and how to incorporate multiple strips of wool to give the appearance of open space in the design. Once the shapes were placed, I tacked them down on the linen, then I hooked #3-, 4-, and 8-cut wool strips to fill anywhere there was a void.

I did most of the design by sight rather than planning it out, since Laura and I were working on the projects concurrently. Laura shared some of the colors she was going to use and how the outline looked on a cream and gold background. By not planning the hamsa design, I had the freedom to just create different quillies and put them together like a puzzle; it was not until most of the space was filled that I made standing wool shapes that fit those spaces. I also used quillies in the background to reflect the main design and to give the background a different texture. I am not a high hooker, so the standing-wool shapes gave my loops room to expand and not curl my linen.

My finished rug will be a wall hanging because of the white background, size, and my uncertainty about how the quillies will hold up with wear.

Here are some parting thoughts on using standing wool in a hooked rug project: 1) So that hooked loops do not overlap the quillies, use wool strips that are about as wide as the loops are tall; 2) Quillies really need to be tacked down well so they do not pop out of your design!

—Gwen Soult

Author's Note

Quilling is the art of rolling narrow strips of paper into circles and other shapes. These shapes are then glued together to form beautiful filigree designs. Popular in Europe during the eighteenth century, quilling was brought to America during colonial times. Standing wool shapes (popularly called quillies) were made into rugs as another way of reusing worn fabric. The strips were rolled, shaped, and then sewn together. Often the quillies were then sewn onto a background fabric for stability.

Hamsa in quilled paper, 12" x 12" framed.. Designed and created by Laura Ouladdaoud, Wayne, Pennsylvania, 2021.

Quilling, *16½" x 16½", #8-cut wool for hooked section and standing wool. Designed and hooked by Gwen Soult, Newport, Pennsylvania, 2021.*

Woodcarving Inspiration: He's My Brother, From Another Mother—a Fiber Mother

I acquired this local woodcarving when we moved to Virginia. The wood has quite the patina, it is hand-carved, and I wish I had more information. Making a companion for him was challenging and fun. I drew the pattern by shining light on the carving and tracing his shadow on brown paper, and then I traced his shape on linen.

Textured wools work wonderfully in the chickens. The eyes, comb, beak, and wattle were pulled from my noodle bin, and the body is hooked in #8 cuts.

Once the hooking was complete, I trimmed away the foundation except for 1½", cut a corresponding shape from a complementary woolen fabric, then stuffed him with fiberfill and blanket-stitched him together with wool yarn. I added wire framework to the tail for stability and pushed a wooden dowel into the head area. The chicken sits atop an antique masher, so I left the bottom open for the masher handle. Since the chicken is only viewed from the front, there was no need to hook the back. Inspiration can be found everywhere; we just need to look.

— Nancy Zeppelin Parcels

He's My Brother, *21" tall, #8-cut wool on linen. Designed and hooked by Nancy Zeppelin Parcels, Rustburg, Virginia, 2017.*

Inspirational woodcarving

Inspiration: Coffee Mug

I made this rug for a dear friend. She offers me her "bed & breakfast" no matter when I'm in her neck of the woods, and it was time to show my appreciation for her friendship. She is a cat lover and drinks tea every morning from her sweet cat mug. When she wasn't in the kitchen, I took a photo of that mug and saw the name of the artist. I contacted the artist via Facebook and she gave me permission to use her art to hook a rug. She even sent me a copy of the original drawing.

I enlarged the artwork at an office supply store to make it easier to see, then I drew my version on the linen. I made the birds bigger in scale since the detail would have been hard to hook in my preferred #8 cut. I eliminated other details that weren't essential to the story. (I inadvertently eliminated one detail and really wanted to add it in, but once the area was already hooked, I decided it was not worth the trouble. I'm not going to reveal the error because most people don't notice, but if they do, it's my prerogative as an artist to leave out anything I want. After all, Magdalena omitted feet on her birds!)

I designed this rug for my friend's kitchen, but since she has those cats, she decided to frame it and hang it elsewhere in her house. A master woodworker made the frame and fashioned a wooden matting that exactly fit around my wonky binding. Although the matting accentuates the wavy edges, I think this adds a bit of whimsy and I love it! The mug is proudly displayed on a shelf above the rug, and I have a feeling it isn't used nearly as much as it was before it inspired that rug.

The lesson here: If you want to hook something for a friend, you can't go wrong by checking out the art in their home to find an idea that will make them happy.

—Kathleen Eckhaus

The Cat's Meow, 35" x 22½", #8-cut wool on linen.
Design adapted from the artwork of Debi Hron and hooked by Kathleen Eckhaus, Elliottsburg, Pennsylvania, 2019.
The inspiration mug in its place of honor with the hooked rug.

Inspiration: Tiles

This tile comes from the Spanish town of Manises, where beautiful, brightly colored tiles decorate many of the town's buildings.

Although this tile is not one of the more colorful ones, I was drawn to it because I love birds. This design has a whimsical feeling that I wanted to interpret into a hooked mat—or two. I love the long legs and the off-balance bird being held up by heart- and leaf-shaped motifs.

Like many rug hookers, I have way too many hooked rugs rolled up and stored away. For this project, I wanted to hook something that I could use, so I used the tile as inspiration for round placemats for the dining table. The dark blue-and-brown palette works well with my dishes and the warm hue of the antique wood tabletop.

Since I wanted to keep the primitive look of the design, I traced a dinner plate on the linen, then drew each design separately.

—Karen Larsen

Dinner Time, 13" diameter, #8-cut wool on linen. Designed and hooked by Karen Larsen, Elliottsburg, Pennsylvania, 2020.

KATHLEEN ECKHAUS

Handmade tile from Manises, Spain

116 | Hooked on Handwork

Inspiration: Medieval Tiles

The inspiration for this design came from a rug hooking class on medieval tiles taught by Cindy MacIntosh in Nova Scotia, Canada. Cindy provided a variety of patterns to choose from. The actual tile designs were 6" squares. These types of designs are hundreds of years old and readily available in specialty books and online with no copyright issues.

I chose four different squares for the pillow design. Traditionally, this style of medieval tile was only produced in two colors with high contrast. I decided to follow the plan and hook my rug with two colors, so my only decision was whether the motif or the background should be light.

In addition to the pillow, I created a wall hanging in the same style, also inspired by beautiful medieval tiles. These were easy designs to put on the linen and to hook.

—Tanya McNutt

Medieval Tile Pillow, 14" x 14", #4-cut wool on linen. Designed and hooked by Tanya McNutt, Truro, Nova Scotia, Canada, 2020.

Medieval Tile Wall Hanging, 8" x 30", #4-cut wool on linen. Designed and hooked by Tanya McNutt, Truro, Nova Scotia, Canada, 2020.

Inspiration: Islamic Geometric Tiles

Geometric patterns are the most common form of architectural artwork throughout the Middle East. Typically, designs are a single geometric motif that is repeated. Craftspeople have been molding concrete, shaping mosaic tiles, and painting geometric artwork for thousands of years, and it is still practiced today. Featured in all parts of Abu Dhabi city, decorative panels are found in mosques, palaces, hotels, malls, and government buildings.

This rug is based on a 12-point star pattern prevalent in Abu Dhabi. The central motif could be repeated to create a bigger rug. However, in this piece, the connecting points are omitted, and individual rosettes flank the main motif.

—Ti Seymour

Islamic Geometric, *16" x 30", #4- and 5-cut wool on linen. Designed and hooked by Ti Seymour, Abu Dhabi, UAE, 2020.*

Inspiration: Stained Glass

I made a stained glass–style mat to complement a lamp and stained-glass panel I already owned. I found a pattern in *Prairie Designs for Stained Glass Windows: 10th Anniversary Edition*, by Alex Spatz (Cliffside Studio, 2003). Use of the designs by "stained glass enthusiasts" is permitted. Drawing the pattern was the most challenging part of this project. The design in the book was a 1"= 6" scale. I needed to change that to fit the bench where I intended to place the mat. I used 1"= 4" scale, and then played a bit. Making all the conversions was interesting because many of the measurements were inches plus fractions. The final design is a bit longer and not quite as wide as it would be if it were completely true to the proportions of the original. I figured this would be fine—it is my bench, after all! I drew the design on linen using a permanent marker and a ruler, tracing a circle for the one round element. I was careful to keep my lines straight on the grain of the linen.

I chose colors that coordinated with the items I owned. Most of the wool strips are a #6 cut. I also used wool velvet, wool yarn, and silk strips. The wool strips for the stained glass's leading, which outlines the sections, is dark purple. I hooked the outlines before filling in the panes, completing a segment of the mat at a time instead of hooking the entire outline. Spot-dyed wool makes some sections look like stained glass. Another challenge was balancing the colors throughout the mat, because there are so many sections. It was important to plan ahead in order to attain this balance—and to remain flexible as changes were needed.

—Gloria McPherson

Stained glass inspiration

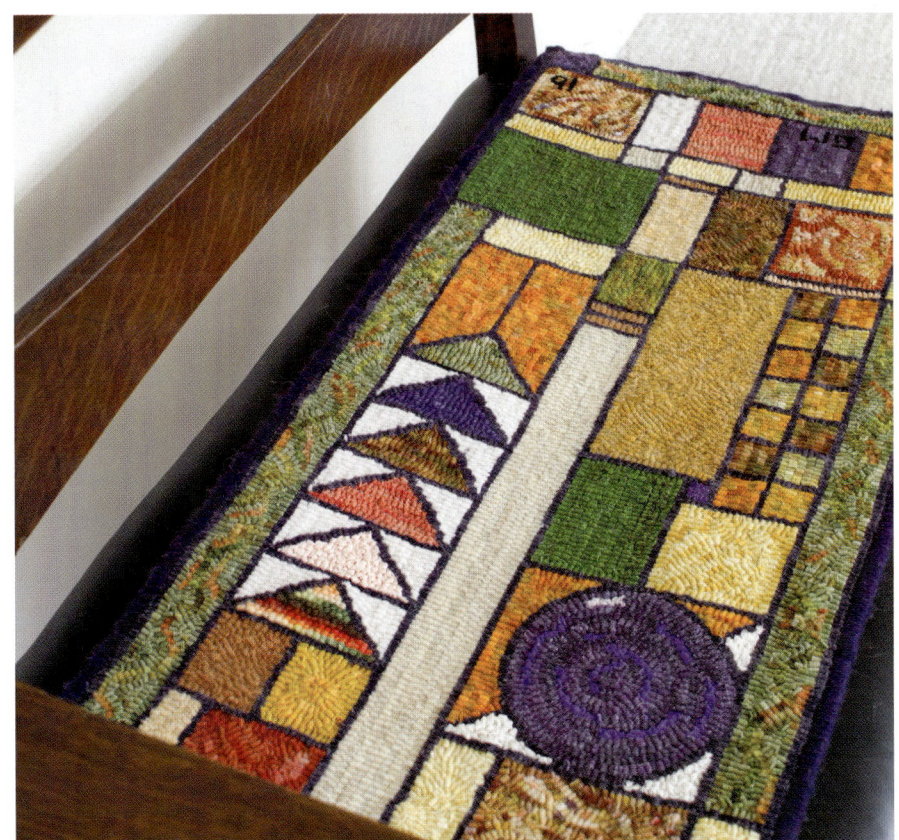

Stained Glass Mat, *16" x 34½", #6-cut wool on linen with wool velvet, wool yarn, and silk strips. Designed and hooked by Gloria McPherson, New Bloomfield, Pennsylvania, 2016.*

Inspiration: Shosoin

When I was in elementary school, I saw my mother latch-hooking a rug. After I became an adult, I learned about rug hooking and my memories were awakened. I met my teacher, Chizuko, seven years ago. I studied and practiced my craft and now I am a McGown Certified Instructor.

The rug I designed is based on a treasure in the Shosoin Repository, a building in the city of Nara that was built in the eighth century. This was an ancient, red-painted ivory shaku, or a measuring tool, that equals approximately 12" in length. I fell in love with the beautiful designs, especially the deer with its flowering horn, the beautiful, figured bird, and the white horse with flowers.

—Yoshiho Nara

*We were unable to obtain a photo of the shaku, but you can see it at:
https://shosoin.kunaicho.go.jp/treasures/?id=0000010034&index=0*

Shosoin, *28½" x 45", #3-cut wool on linen. Designed and hooked by Yoshiho Nara, Tokyo, Japan.*

Inspiration: Hannunvaakuna

The hannunvaakuna is a looped square design that dates back centuries in Finland. The literal translation is (Saint) John's Coat of Arms. It was often carved or painted on buildings or household objects as a good-luck charm. There are many variations of this design in Finland, mostly used in jewelry but also found on coins, buttons, and tattoos. When it is displayed on a street sign, it usually indicates a historic site or a place of interest.

To maintain the simplicity of the design I used just three colors with high contrast. I chose a very dark background and two different values of gold for the symbol. The looped part of the design was hooked in a #9 cut. I hooked the loops with a little extra space in between the rows so I could squeeze in a #4-cut strip of the dark background to accentuate all the curved and overlapping lines. The runes, or symbols, behind the double-loop square were hooked in a slightly darker gold to give a little added depth to the design.

I gave my original hannunvaakuna mat as a hostess gift to my Finnish friend when we visited her and her family in 2018. She graciously displayed it on her dining table with a bowl of delicious Finnish chocolate biscuits.

—Kris Miller

Inspiration jewelry

Hannunvaakuna, 9" x 9", #4- and 9-cut wool on linen. Designed and hooked by Kris Miller, Howell, Michigan, 2018.

9 Inspiration from The Gambia

Art is not what you see, but what you make others see.
— Edgar Degas

Most rug hookers I know have frames, cutters, and multiple hooks. Some of them use primarily recycled fabric, but many purchase beautiful wools, either off-the-bolt or hand-dyed. The rug hookers featured in this chapter make do with what they have on hand—and many of them can't even see their work! I hope that learning about the Rug Aid project will inspire you to set aside any doubts you may have about designing. I suspect that all of us are capable of more than we know.

Heather Ritchie is one of Britain's most experienced rug makers and teachers of rug hooking. In late 2004, when she visited the island of Zanzibar in East Africa, local women and children were fascinated when she demonstrated the simple technique of rug hooking—using recycled local material, clothes, yarn, and plastic bags—and they quickly picked it up.

After returning to the UK, Heather and two friends set up Rug Aid, a non-profit social enterprise. Their goal was to make a difference in some of the poorest communities in Africa—to provide people with the opportunity to bring about change in their lives through the sale of handmade rugs from recycled materials.

Heather learned that begging had recently been outlawed in The Gambia, a move which deprived many blind adults of their only source of income; very few of them had been able to go to school as children so they did not have the skills needed to hold down a job. After learning of the new problem this already-underprivileged group faced, Heather specifically chose to work with people with visual impairments. Rug Aid's first project started at The Gambia Organization of the Visually Impaired (GOVI) School in Serrekunda. She thought she would be almost exclusively teaching women and children, but when she arrived for her first workshop session, she found to her delight that the students were a mixed group of men and women.

Since rug making is a tactile skill, a blind student can create a random-patterned rug. After they have mastered the technique, they will need little help to fill in a complex and beautiful design based on local motifs if a sighted person hooks or prods the outline onto the backing and sorts the fabric into colors.

Rug Aid trainees in The Gambia make rugs and wall hangings that they are encouraged to sell direct and locally. They have added income for their families and a sense of pride in their accomplishments.

In addition, Rug Aid encourages people to draw on the stories of their lives—families, animals, friends, transport, homes, schools—as well as the colors, patterns, and textures of their environments, both rural and urban, to produce beautiful and marketable works of art which bring pleasure to both the creator and the purchaser. The project harnesses the artistic skills people already have and inspires them, even when they are not sure that they have any artistic talent, to express themselves through colors and patterns.

Inspiration is All Around Us

This final chapter is not about designs inspired by other fiber arts. It is simply included for general inspiration. If you are able to see the world around you and have access to the tools you need to design and hook a rug, then I hope you will be encouraged by these artists from The Gambia who have limited sight and only simple tools. They make do with what they have in their communities. Some of the Gambian hookers are not even aware of the colors of their materials, but they have learned to hook rugs—and they have learned to love rug hooking. Reading their story encouraged me to let go a little bit more and allow myself to enjoy the process and love the result. Thanks, Rug Aid, for the inspiration.

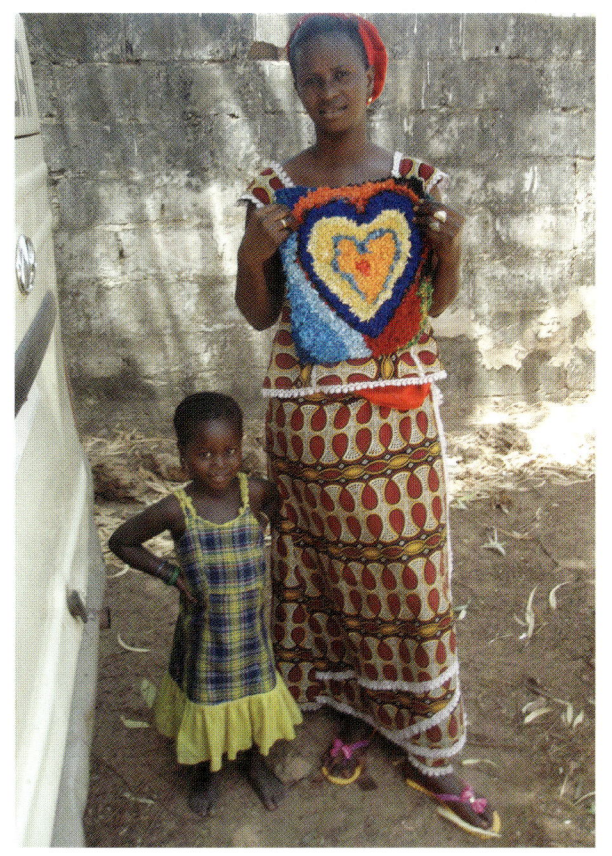

This is is Isatu. She is sighted but attends the Rug Aid workshop to make rugs to sell to support her blind parents.

Ernest is the manager. He is totally blind but does an amazing job running the programs and sorting out all the students. He also makes rugs.

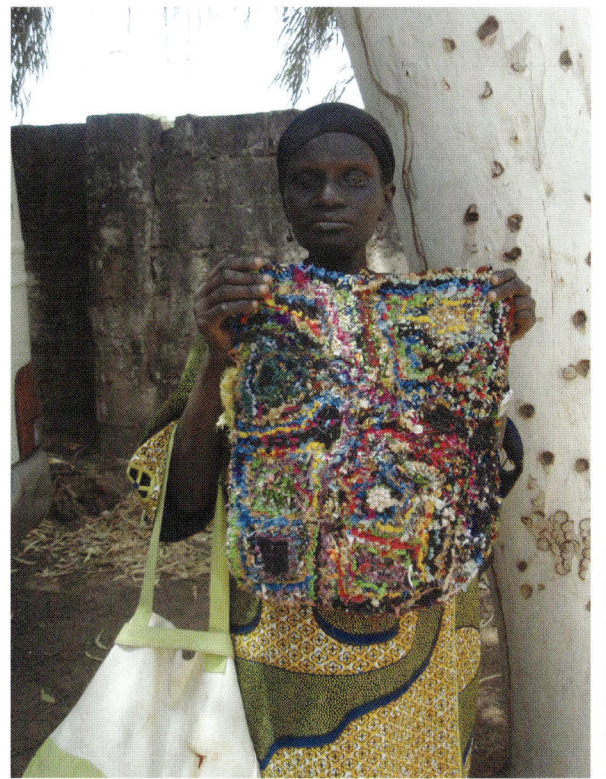

Senabu makes incredible rugs. Her family finds her the fabrics and cuts them for her, then she picks strips at random and hooks them into rugs. Senabu is totally blind.

Babacu is a helper who finds the colors required and cuts them up for the students. He has a little sight.

Conclusion

Don't worry about mistakes. Making things out of mistakes, that's creativity. — Peter Max

I've always loved that quote. Peter Max is a German American artist who is known for his bright colors and cheerful designs. I like to think that he doesn't worry too much about mistakes but just incorporates them into his art. I think I will add his advice to my notes to share with new rug hookers when I teach a class. We do need to stop worrying about mistakes!

In our culture, we have this notion that only some of us can sing and some of us can dance and some of us are artistic. But the truth is, we are all musical and we can all draw, it's just that we do these things differently. Some of us sing our own tunes in our own way, like Bob Dylan, and some of us have a simplistic style of drawing, like Grandma Moses and Magdalena Briner Eby. Yes, there are rug hookers who design a rug that looks like a photograph and others who prefer the primitive look of a child's drawing. All styles are acceptable. All styles are art.

Many rug hookers are already getting inspiration from other textile and visual arts, but perhaps the ideas in this book will give you some fresh places to look, different ways to change a pattern to make it your own, and new motivation for choosing your colors.

I don't know about you, but I never get tired of looking at the work of other rug hookers. I pick up old *Rug Hooking* magazines and enjoy them over and over. I look through my rug-hooking books and think about new designs that I want to create.

If you are a confident designer, I hope you got some new ideas from the rugs in this book. If you have never designed a rug before, I hope you will have the confidence to give it a try. Be sure to put your initials and the date on every rug you hook because someday your rugs will be family heirlooms.

Have fun designing rugs that look like paintings, rugs that are color-planned with beautiful shading, or rugs that are just quirky. Don't be afraid to put that marker to your linen. You can always grab another color marker if you change your mind. If worse comes to worse, flip the linen over because there's a whole blank side on the back so you can start again. No one will ever know.

Make this the day that you design something new. Look around you for inspiration. Hook a rug!

Resources and References

Better Homes and Gardens. *Traditional American Crafts*. Des Moines, Iowa: Meredith Corporation, 1988.

Gilbert, Janet. "A Brief History of Sunbonnet Sue." *Classic Sewing Magazine*, Fall 2016, 65-70, *classicsewingmagazine.com*.

Hieronimus, Ingrid. *Special Effects Using Creative Stitches*. Self-published by Ingrid Hieronimus, 2014.

Jamar, Tracy. *Coils, Folds, Twists, and Turns: Contemporary Techniques in Fiber*. Guilford, CT: Stackpole Books, 2017.

Lawrence, Evelyn and Kathy Wright. *Rug Hooking Traditions with Magdalena Briner Eby*. Oxford, OH: Traditions by Wright & Co., 2011.

Makhan, Rosemary. *Floral Abundance: Appliqué Designs Inspired by William Morris*. Bothell, WA, 2000: That Patchwork Place®.

MacKinnon, Colleen. https://pennyrugsandmore.blogspot.com

Pavich, Tamara. *Designed by You: Ideas and Inspiration for Rug Hookers*. Northbrook, IL: Ampry Publishing LLC, 2017.

Peck, Amelia. "American Needlework in the Eighteenth Century." In *Heilbrunn Timeline of Art History*. New York: The Metropolitan Museum of Art, (October 2003), http://www.metmuseum.org/toah/hd/need/hd_need.htm.

Rug Aid, http://www.rug-aid.org/index.html

Rug Hooking Magazine, www.rughookingmagazine.com

Rug Hooking Magazine, ed. *Finishing Hooked Rugs, Favorite Techniques from the Experts*. Mechanicsburg, PA: Rug Hooking Magazine, 2013.

Open Access Artwork

Ellen Banker was the first contributor to send images that were in the public domain from The Metropolitan Museum of Art in New York City, and she introduced me to their Open Access Artwork.

The Met provides high-resolution images that you can download. As part of the Met's Open Access policy, you can freely copy, modify, and distribute Open Access images, even for commercial purposes.

Explore Creative Commons, which is an international network "devoted to educational access and expanding the range of creative works available for others to build upon legally and to share." (Wikipedia)

Look for these symbols.

List of Contributing Artists

Ania Knap, Reading, Massachusetts. Ania is a McGown Certified Instructor and recovering scientist whose passion for vibrant colors drives her artistic creativity. Her PhD in chemistry and artist's view combine to define her unique approach to symmetry, contrast, and color. Follow her on the rug hooking blog she publishes in collaboration with her daughter, Monique Frechette, entitled, *My Mother's a Hooker*.

Brigitte Webb, Dingwall, Scotland. Brigitte first learned about rug hooking on a trip to Nova Scotia. She is largely self-taught and has produced more than 250 pieces from 2" to 10' in size. She has had articles and rugs featured in over 20 publications including *Rug Hooking* magazine, Celebration, and various hooking books. There are few rug hookers in her corner of Scotland so she is teaching and promoting the craft wherever she goes.

Chizuko Hayami, Tokyo, Japan. Chizuko learned rug hooking when she lived in New York with her family from 1989 to 1994. She is a McGown Certified Instructor and has a studio where she teaches many newer styles, such as the reverse hooking she used in her rug. View some of her original designs at https://rughook.com/collections/designs-by-chizuko-hayami and learn more about her and what she does at her website, https://rug-hooking883.jimdo.com. Site is in Japanese with some English translation.

Christie Yorks, Mexico, Pennsylvania. Christie is a full-time health field worker. Two grown daughters and four grandchildren keep Christie and her husband busy. Her free time is consumed with a good book, an exercise class, a walk with her golden retriever, a session at the sewing machine piecing a quilt, or sitting down to do handwork and taking in a good television show. She has added rug hooking to her free time activities.

Debra Smith, Landisburg, Pennsylvania, is a rug hooker and fiber-art enthusiast living in south central Pennsylvania. She is currently most interested in embroidery and rug hooking, though she has dabbled in quilting, tatting, crochet, and many other needle arts. A member of Magdalena Rug Hookers, ATHA, and TIGHR, she enjoys traveling to gatherings of rug hookers around the country and around the world. From 2009 to 2022 she was editor of *Rug Hooking* magazine, which she considers the best job in the world.

Elaine Montambeau first learned to hook rugs 15 years ago from her mother-in-law, Joy Harvey. She enjoys creating objects that can be used day-to-day, which is one of the reasons she loves rug hooking. Elaine's educational background is in graphic and information design which, she believes, is why she is drawn to the detailed work that can be done using fine shading.

Ellen Banker, Williamsburg, Virginia, holding her rug *Chief Feline Officer*, lives in Virginia. Her original rug designs are known for their whimsy and charm and many have appeared in *Rug Hooking* magazine. She is the author of *Hooked on Words*, published by Ampry Publishing in 2018.

Francie Appleman, Turbotville, Pennsylvania, is a retired nurse who just sold the farm and moved to a smaller house in town. She and her husband had a grain farm with corn, soybeans, and hay, and they also had turkeys, chickens, and a flock of sheep. Francie is hoping that with less outdoor work she will have more time to spend with her eight grandchildren and doing the fun fiber hobbies she loves, including weaving, spinning, knitting, sewing, quilting, and her newest passion, rug hooking.

Gloria McPherson, New Bloomfield, Pennsylvania, has been hooking for several years. She often makes her own patterns, using photos she has taken or other things in her life for inspiration. She wrote an article for RHM and is a member of Magdalena Rug Hookers. She also enjoys punch-needle hooking, quilting, and other fiber arts. Her idea of a super vacation is to travel and learn more about one of her interests.

Gwen Soult, Newport, Pennsylvania, runs a commercial dairy goat operation; two years ago she took a rug hooking course through her local arts council and was hooked! She has always liked fiber arts from her days in school but dabbled in many until she discovered rug hooking. Suddenly something clicked and she now has a new passion! She already has a stash of wool that will last her for a couple of years.

Håkon Grøn Hensvold, Skreia, Norway, is a teacher in arts and crafts with a specialty in textiles. He loves to garden and collects hoyas. He lives in a small village called Skreia that lies 12 Norwegian miles north of Oslo. He hopes that his three-year-old grandson will someday wear that handmade sweater that was his rug inspiration.

Joanne Page, Wake Forest, North Carolina, is the owner and designer for Woolly Worms Rugs. She has contributed to *Rug Hooking* magazine, *Wool Works* magazine and *Punch Needle & Primitive Stitcher* magazine. She lives in North Carolina with her husband of 33 years. After 23 years of homeschooling, she hopes to continue teaching and develop her line of rug hooking patterns.

Julia Majury, Elliottsburg, Pennsylvania, began her fiber-art journey with her grandmother teaching her to crochet when she was five, then her mom teaching her to sew, and then joining the cross-stitch club in junior high. Through the years, Julia has taken up quilting, fabric collage and painting, embroidery, wool appliqué, punch needle, Sashiko, knitting, spinning, rug hooking, and weaving.

Karen Larsen, Elliottsburg, Pennsylvania, has used her BA in art to design and create traditional hooked rugs since 2006. She has had many articles published in *Rug Hooking* magazine, including her snowy owl design on the cover of the Nov/Dec 2012 issue. Her magpie design is the cover of the book *Rug Hooking Through the Year* (Ampry Publishing LLC, 2018). Birds and nature frequent her original designs.

Kris Miller, Howell, Michigan, started rug hooking in 1998. She specializes in primitive designs with an emphasis on textured wool and wide cuts. The owner of Spruce Ridge Studios, she has won many awards and ribbons for her hooked rugs. She is the author of *Introduction to Rug Hooking* (*Rug Hooking* Magazine, 2015). She has taught at many rug camps across the United States and internationally in Finland and England. Kris lives on a small farm in Michigan with her husband and an assortment of sheep, alpacas, an angora goat, and a dog. Find her at www.spruceridgestudios.com

Kyoko Okamura, Ube, Yamaguchi, Japan, first learned about rug hooking from a friend. She immediately fell in love with it and was referred to Chizuko's Studio in Tokyo. She has been hooking for 19 years, is a member of Chizuko Rug Hooking Studio and the McGown Guild, and is a McGown Certified Instructor.

Lin Keller, Shermans Dale, Pennsylvania, started hooking about 10 years ago after joining the Magdalena Rug Hookers of Perry County, Pennsylvania. The group meets monthly at a local fiber shop and works on projects while solving the world's problems. Lin's first love for creative expression is quilting, which she has enjoyed for over 20 years. She also dabbles in wool appliqué, embroidery, and mixed-media collage.

Liz Gordon, Lexington, Virginia, is a retired writer for national magazines, including *Rug Hooking*, and has hooked more than 100 medium-sized and large rugs and several wall hangings. Liz often mixes sari silks, yarns, and velvets into her wool rugs, and she loves the process of choosing just the right colors. Many of her rugs have gone to church and dog-rescue auctions.

Nancy Zeppelin Parcels, Rustburg, Virginia, began her rug hooking journey with a simple 8" x 8" burlap mat in 1999. Working on her own for almost two years taught her many valuable lessons. She met her mentor, Yvonne Miller, a McGown Certified Instructor who shared stories, dyeing knowledge, color knowledge, and taught Nancy how to fine shade. Nancy attended McGown teacher's training and graduated in 2007. She loves teaching and traveling to share her love of color and rug hooking with her students.

Peg McPherson, New Bloomfield, Pennsylvania, has been crocheting for approximately 43 years. She started working on projects so she didn't have to pay attention to the football games that her husband watched. Peg has been rug hooking since 2014, when two friends suggested that they could teach her, and she enjoyed pulling those loops. Recently retired, she has limited her hobbies to rug hooking and crochet; however, she did say she might try punch needle one of these days. She also loves to work in her flower gardens.

Rachel Lea Olendorf Beaston, Blain, Pennsylvania, was introduced to rug hooking about two years ago when a friend at church showed her pictures of finished projects. That friend invited Rachel to join a group of rug hookers that met once a month, and that was the beginning. She got her starter kit and went to her first (but not her last) meeting. The large rug in this book is her second project, and she has learned a lot from hooking it. She's looking forward to designing her next rug and hopes to incorporate her love of nature into it.

Sirpa Ojala, Pomarkku, Finland, is a visual artist whose primary inspiration is nature. She lives in the middle of a forest with a lake nearby, and these environments are prevalent in her artwork. She is a member of the Pori Society of Artists and is an active participant in group expositions. She also has private exhibitions of her work twice a year. Her main artistic techniques are gouache, acrylic, and aquarelle painting, rug hooking, and ceramics.

Stephanie Allen-Krauss, Montpelier, Vermont, is a fourth-generation rug hooker who learned the techniques at age six from her mother, Anne Ashworth, a nationally-known rug-hooking teacher. She also learned about dyeing wool fabric and repairing antique hooked rugs. She currently owns Green Mountain Hooked Rugs, an online store and retail shop in Montpelier, Vermont. During her career, Stephanie has held offices in local, national, and international rug-hooking guilds, and in 2010, she was honored with the Governor's Heritage Award as best traditional artist in the state of Vermont.

Susan Kesler-Simpson, Danville, Pennsylvania, earned her BS and MA degrees in textiles at the University of Nebraska-Lincoln. She is an avid weaver and author of four weaving books. Another will be released soon.

Tanya McNutt, Truro, Nova Scotia, Canada, is a retired laboratory technologist who began rug hooking after her retirement in 2006. She has used wool fabric, yarn, ribbons, sari silk, and other fibers in her pieces and is always interested in new techniques and using alternate materials. Some of the designs she uses are her own, and many others are purchased from commercial rug-pattern designers.

Ti Seymour has lived in Abu Dhabi, UAE, for 18 years, bar a five-year stint in Montreal where rug hooking was introduced. Nine years—and teaching certifications in rug hooking and Oxford Punch Needle—later, she is working toward a college diploma in fiber arts. A craftsperson at heart, Ti believes that where there's a will to create, there's a craft to investigate.

Tracy Granger lives in the Pocono Mountains of Pennsylvania and has nature's inspiration at her back door. She is a retired custom picture framer/gallery owner, and her journey into rug hooking was a natural extension from years of textile framing. She finds great comfort while hooking geometric rugs with their straight lines and repetitive motion. Whether designing, color planning, hooking, or traveling, her soul continues to be nurtured.

Yoshiho Nara is a McGown Certified Instructor from Tokyo, Japan. She started rug hooking at Chizuko Rug Hooking Studio seven years ago. Yoshiho recognizes many beautiful designs in the art of Japan and hopes to continue to investigate them through rug hooking.

Please Accept or Decline Your Book Club Benefits!

Dear Rug Hooker,

Please review the benefits of Book Club membership, and **join the *Rug Hooking* Book Club today!** We typically publish 4 books per year. And when you join now, we will send your **FIRST** book for an exclusive discount: only $9.95 USD, plus shipping and handling. That's HUGE savings for new Book Club members... more than 60% off the regular price! **Look at the benefits you'll receive:**

✓ **Guaranteed discounts on new books**	✓ **Special sales only for book club members**
✓ **Go green! Hassle-free automatic book payments**	✓ **A free E-Newsletter with book club members-only content**
✓ **Monthly discounts on our online store**	✓ **First access to our newest books**

BONUS! Special one-time discount off your first book!

RETAIL PRICE*

~~$28.95~~ USD

BOOK CLUB PRICE*

~~$22.95~~ USD

YOUR EXCLUSIVE PRICE

$9.95 USD

To learn more about the *Rug Hooking* Book Club and become a Book Club Member today:

 https://www.rughookingmagazine.com/RBC995

 (877) 297 - 0965 (U.S.) or
(866) 375-8626 (Canada)

Exclusive offer for new Book Club members only!

Retail and Book Club prices can vary with each title.